The Romans in Lunesdale

by

David Shotter and Andrew White

Centre for North-West Regional Studies
University of Lancaster
1995

The Romans in Lunesdale
by David Shotter and Andrew White

This volume is the thirty-first in a series published by the Centre for North-West Regional Studies at the University of Lancaster. Details of titles which are still available may be obtained from the Centre.

ISSN 0308-4310

Published by the Centre for North-West Regional Studies, University of Lancaster, 1995

Typeset in Linotype Stempel Garamond by Carnegie Publishing Ltd, 18 Maynard St, Preston, Lancs.
Printed and bound in the UK by The Alden Press, Oxford

British Library Cataloguing in Publication Data
A CIP record for this book is available from the British Library

ISBN 0-901800-68-6

Contents

	List of illustrations	iv
	Acknowledgements	vi
	Introduction	1
1	The Lune Valley; environment and history	3
2	Roman Conquest and Occupation	10
3	Lancaster	18
4	Burrow-in-Lonsdale	36
5	Low Borrow Bridge	47
6	Roads, Industry and Farmers (with a section on excavations of roads)	58
7	The Later Years	77
8	Conclusion	83
	Appendices	
	I Portus Setantiorum	85
	II List of selected dates	88
	III Inscriptions from Lunesdale	89
	Abbreviations	109
	Bibliography	109

List of Illustrations

Front cover Reconstruction drawing of the Roman fort at Low Borrow Bridge. (David Vale)
1. Map of the Lune Valley .
2. Aerial photograph looking southwards down the Lune gorge.
3. Aerial photograph of the Lune estuary from 50,000 feet.
4. The Vale of Lonsdale.
5. Maps to illustrate Roman campaigns in the north-west.
6. Roman marching-camp at Rey Cross on Stainmore.
7. Reconstruction by David Vale of the Roman fort of Lancaster.
8. Agricolan rampart, Lancaster.
9. Plan of the successive Roman forts at Lancaster.
10. Timber-lined well, Lancaster.
11. Bronze diploma, Malpas.
12. Plan of Lancaster showing the fort and related civilian settlement.
13. Bath-suite of the courtyard building in Vicarage Field, Lancaster.
14. Detail of the bath-suite, Lancaster.
15. Fort bath-house, Lancaster.
16. Shop in *vicus*, Lancaster.
17. Group of Roman statuary, Lancaster.
18. Tombstone of a former trooper of the *Ala Sebosiana* from Worms on the Rhine.
19. Professor Ian Richmond, Lancaster, 1950.
20. Hoard of third-century coins, Lancaster.
21. Reconstruction drawing of the Roman fort of Burrow-in-Lonsdale.
22. Engraving of Burrow Hall.
23. Aerial photograph of Burrow Hall.
24. Plan of the fort at Burrow-in-Lonsdale.
25. Excavations at Burrow-in-Lonsdale, 1952-3.
26. Excavations at Burrow-in-Lonsdale, 1952-3.
27. South gateway, Burrow-in-Lonsdale.
28. Bronze horse-trapping, Overtown.
29. Bronze ox-head escutcheon, Burrow-in-Lonsdale.
30. Carved capital, Burrow-in-Lonsdale.
31. Lancaster & Carlisle Railway in the Lune gorge, 1846.
32. Excavations of 1883, Low Borrow Bridge.
33. Aerial photographs of Low Borrow Bridge.

34. Reconstruction of the fort at Low Borrow Bridge.
35. Bath-house, Low Borrow Bridge.
36. Cemetery at Low Borrow Bridge, excavated 1991.
37. Tombstone of Aelia Sentica, Low Borrow Bridge.
38. Norman motte-and-bailey castle, Tebay.
39. Roman milestone, Caton.
40. Roman milestone, Middleton.
41. Map of Roman roads in the Lune Valley.
42. Section through Roman road, Leck.
43. Section through Roman road, Leck.
44. Tile-kiln, Quernmore.
45. Pottery from Quernmore kilns.
46. Roman lime-kiln, Quernmore.
47. Roman altar from Weardale.
48. Altar to Jalonus Contrebis.
49. Farmstead at Claughton.
50. Farmstead at Sellet Hall.
51. Farmsteads and fields at Eller Beck.
52. Farmstead and possible signal station at Middleton.
53. Detail of statue, Lancaster.
54. Wery Wall, Lancaster.
55. Wery Wall, Lancaster.
56. Wall and bastion at Caer Gybi, Holyhead.
57. Roman altar, *RIB* 600.
58. Roman altar, *RIB* 601.
59. Roman altar, *RIB* 602.
60. Roman dedication slab, *RIB* 604.
61. Roman dedication slab, *RIB* 605.
62. Roman dedication slab, Lancaster.
63. Lead sealing, Lancaster.
64. Roman altar, *RIB* 610.
65. Roman tombstone, *RIB* 611.
66. Roman tombstone, *RIB* 612.
67. Roman milestone, Caton.

Acknowledgements

THE authors wish to acknowledge the following individuals and organisations for drawings and photographs which have been commissioned for the present work or reproduced from other sources:

John Anstee (35)
Trustees of the British Museum (11)
Council of the Cumberland & Westmorland
Archaeological & Antiquarian Society (24, 32, 65)
B. J. N. Edwards (18, 28, 42, 43)
Paul Gibbons (49)
Geoff Harris (17, 39, 48, 57, 58, 59, 60, 61, 67)
G. D. B.Jones/Manunair (2, 6, 33, 38, 51, 52)
Lancaster City Museums (4, 19, 20, 22, 25, 26, 31, 39, 45, 48, 53, 57, 58, 60, 61, 63, 67)
Lancaster University Archaeological Unit (23, 36, 37, 49, 50)
Peter Lee (5, 9, 12, 37)
Adrian Olivier (23, 49, 50)
Timothy Potter (15, 16)
A. V. Roe & Co. (3)
Society of Antiquaries of London (29)
Stadtarchiv Worms (18)
Paul Thompson/Wendy Moore (1, 5, 24, 27, 41, 47)
David Vale (7, 21, 34 and front cover)

Introduction

The river Lune flows through a landscape of contrasts, rising in the Westmorland fells, crossing into Lancashire in the vicinity of Kirkby Lonsdale, and then running through a widening valley into the sea at Morecambe Bay. Its valley is known today, variously and interchangeably, as 'the Lune valley', 'Lunesdale' and 'Lonsdale', marking the mixed Anglo-Saxon, Norse and Norman origins of its inhabitants.

Socially and economically, its role has been crucial, in early times supporting arable farmers and pastoralists, supplying salt, clay for pottery and tiles, and salmon and sea-trout for eating. In the eighteenth century the river brought great prosperity to the port of Lancaster. The valley was clearly significant also for reasons of military security and communications in the Roman period; three forts were disposed along its length, each commanding a different type of terrain. The garrisons in their turn provided an important economic stimulus for local and immigrant farmers, traders and industrialists, both from the ready market for supplies which they represented and as a result of the lasting peace which they brought.

The purpose of the present book is to review the evidence for occupation in the forts themselves, to see how far they encouraged the growth of settled communities in their own vicinity, and to show how current research-techniques are demonstrating the social breadth of the prosperity that the Roman occupying forces stimulated. Individual sites and areas within the Lune valley have been studied and published; this is the first recent attempt to bring the results of that research together in order to present a broadly-based view of the valley in Roman times.

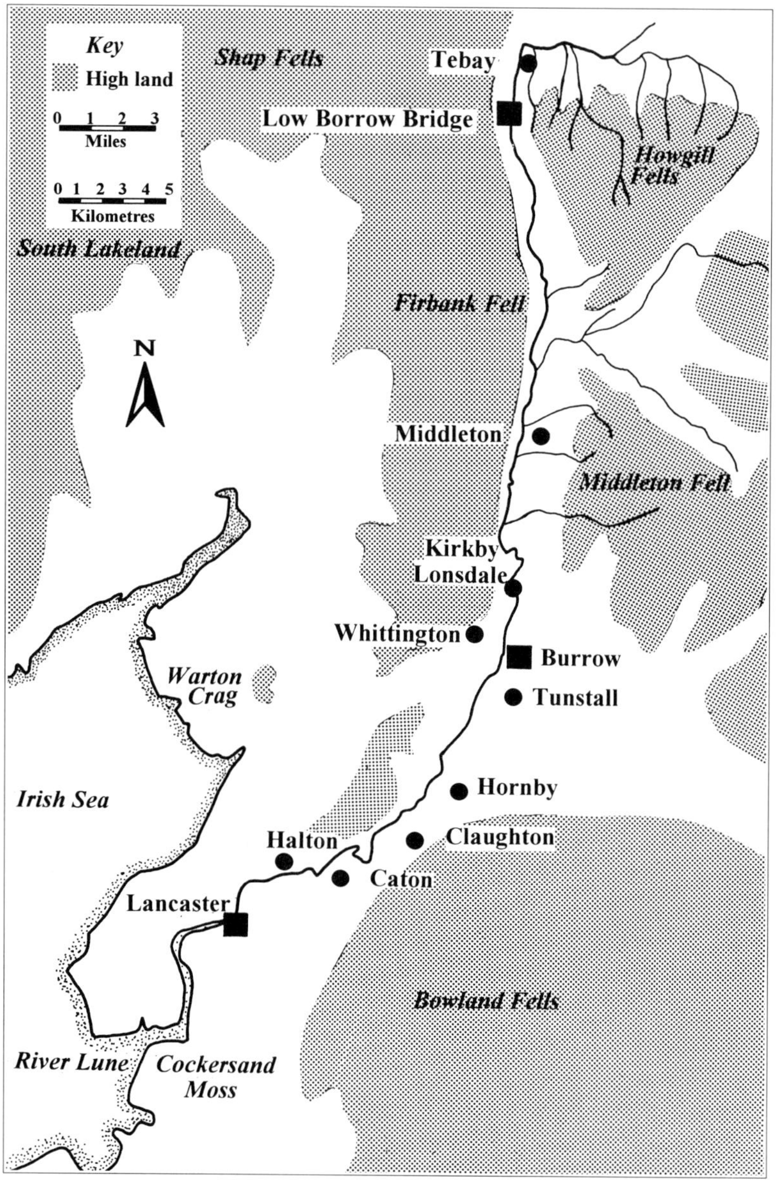

1. Map of the Lune Valley from its source to the sea, showing places mentioned in the text. (P. Thompson./ W. Moore.)

Chapter 1

The Lune Valley: environment and history

THE river Lune rises high on the Howgill Fells near Ravenstonedale in Cumbria. There is some disagreement as to which is the actual source, but the river seems to rise on the slopes of Green Bell, being known first as Dale Beck, then as Greenside Beck, then finally as the Lune from Newbiggin until it enters the Irish Sea some 45 miles to the south-west.[1] Its name cannot be satisfactorily explained; early forms include Loun, Loin, Loyn and Lon, while even today its valley is called either 'Lonsdale' or 'Lunesdale'. We find unconvincing the arguments for a Celtic origin, cognate with the Irish word *slan*, and in all probability the name goes back to that oldest stratum of names in the British countryside, the pre-Celtic.[2]

The course of the Lune can be divided geographically into four main sections:

1. (Ravenstonedale–Tebay). A small beck running first northwards, then more or less westwards through the high fells, fed by a number of other tributaries and gradually becoming a river, then turning sharply south towards

2. (Tebay–Sedbergh). The so-called Lune gorge, where it runs southwards through a dramatic steep-sided valley shared today by the M6 motorway and the main west-coast railway line.

3. (Sedbergh–Caton). The valley then opens out to a broad U-shape from Sedbergh to Lancaster, the most picturesque section being that between Kirkby Lonsdale and Caton. The Lune cuts mostly through glacial drift deposits but on meeting a rocky projection to the north-west of Caton village it makes a very sharp bend at a place called Crook O'Lune.

4. (Skerton–Sunderland Point). At Skerton Weirs, just to the north-east of Lancaster, the river becomes tidal. At Lancaster the Castle Hill, a rocky mass capped with Boulder Clay, causes the river to make a broad loop to the north. Thereafter the course of the estuary winds between salt-marshes and debouches into Morecambe Bay between Glasson Dock and Sunderland Point.

The Lune receives a number of significant tributaries, such as the Rawthey, Dee, Barbon Beck, Leck Beck, Greeta, Wenning and Artle Beck, themselves in some cases the product of several merged tributaries. All these rise on the high ground to the east of the Lune, and have created side valleys which have in turn offered through routes from early times.

Until the last Ice Age the Lune ran southwards at Crook O'Lune, through the Quernmore valley. At that time its route became blocked by glacial moraine. Later the old course was recolonised by the much smaller river Conder which today flows southwards and enters the Lune estuary at Conder Green.[3]

This is entirely a descriptive and geographical account and ignores the effect of the river on later human activity. The Lune itself provides a natural route, adopted by many later roads, in a general north-easterly/south-westerly direction, and also offers an easy route eastwards via its tributaries. Lancaster grew up around the lowest bridging point of the Lune which made it an important route-centre.

The narrow corridor between the sea to the west and hills to the east has always influenced transport; it is no mere accident that the modern A6 road, M6 motorway, Lancaster Canal and main west-coast railway line all run parallel within a few hundred metres of each other through Lancaster. In the Lune gorge the roads and railway line are forced by the steep sides to run parallel in a dramatic fashion through the narrow corridor of available flat ground.

Since the estuary of the Lune is navigable – in the eighteenth century ships up to a maximum of about 400 tons came upriver – the position of Lancaster was doubly significant, standing as it does at the head of the tidal reach. Skerton Weirs are of medieval origin and we do not know the original tidal extent of the river. The Weirs, however, seem to take advantage of natural shallows between a group of small shingle islands which still exist, indicating perhaps that this always represented the limits of the tidal reach.

A single Roman altar from Halton, above the Weirs, is often quoted as evidence that the river was navigable thus far at least in Roman times, because the inscription refers to a unit of boatmen. It seems more likely that the inscription itself was moved from Lancaster to Halton in post-Roman times and therefore cannot be used as evidence.

Although it forms a natural corridor for road traffic in certain directions, the Lune valley also acts as a barrier to traffic in others. Even today there are relatively few bridges across the river (at Lancaster, Halton, Crook O'Lune, Gressingham and Kirkby Lonsdale) and the steepness of the valley sides leaves limited opportunities for creating routes, as it were, across its grain.

Strategically the Romans demanded broadly north-south routes in order first to conquer, and then to hold down, the subject territory,

2. A dramatic low-angle aerial photograph looking southwards down the Lune gorge. Tebay is in the foreground and the Roman fort at Low Borrow Bridge can just be seen at the top right-hand corner. River, railway, motorway and roads all compete for the level ground.
(Photograph by courtesy of G. D. B. Jones/Manunair.)

but upstream of Lancaster this was achieved only with difficulty. The same problem was met in the upper part of the Ribble valley, where the river runs at an angle to the line of advance.

In its lower valley section between Sedbergh and Caton the Lune has clearly moved backwards and forwards across its flood-plain in historic times, in response to winter floods and normal hydrological influences. This can be seen from anomalous parish boundaries, left on the 'wrong' side of the river, reflecting its older courses, and from the dried-up former beds themselves.

In Lancaster as well, the movement may have been quite dramatic and there is reason to believe that the river course in Roman times lay along the line of Damside Street, well to the south of its present line. It is just possible that it split and flowed to both north and south of the island of Green Ayre. The date at which it established its present course is unknown, but since the latest Roman fort in Lancaster, of the mid-fourth century A.D., seems to be aligned to the Damside Street course it seems highly likely that the change was post-Roman. A similar but opposite shift of channel further downstream has left the former island of Salt Ayre high and dry on the north bank.

Land-use in the Lune valley is very varied; in broad terms it now ranges from rough grazing for sheep on the open fells above about 900 feet OD to dairy farming on the lusher meadows in the valley bottom, with further grazing for sheep and cattle on the coastal and estuarine salt-marshes. There is very little arable, though increasingly old grassland is being periodically ploughed up and reseeded. This has an effect on the perceived distribution of the Roman monuments and their preservation. In arable country such as in East Anglia the ploughing up of ancient sites simultaneously reveals them and destroys them. In predominantly pastoral areas, like the Lune valley, sites frequently survive as standing earthworks. Those that do not are virtually undetectable without remote sensing equipment.

In ancient times the pattern of agriculture in this area was probably very different, as we shall see, with less specialisation and more crops such as oats or barley to feed the largely unproductive Roman troops and cavalry horses. Climatic change and altered demands have led to profound changes in the farming economy of this area even since the seventeenth century, so it is not surprising if even larger changes have occurred since the Roman period.

Within the Lune valley are the sites of three Roman forts, reflecting its strategic importance as a route – at Lancaster, Burrow-in-Lonsdale and Low Borrow Bridge. These are linked by roads, but other roads run across the grain of the country providing strategic north-south routes, such as the high-level road between Manchester and Carlisle via Bowland Forest. An unusually large number of milestones survive.

3. Aerial photograph of the Lune estuary from 50,000 feet, looking south-west, taken by A. V. Roe & Co. of Manchester.

Outside each of the forts and under their protection lay civilian settlements which combined comforts for the troops with small merchant communities; in the military north of Britain towns were very few – Carlisle is a rare exception – and settlements outside forts were the main tool for Romanisation of the civilian population. At Lancaster, however, it can be argued that the extra-mural settlement was large and urban in character – in other words it was well on its way to becoming a town.[4]

The subsequent history of these three sites has been very different, reflecting the widely different nature of their locations. The fort at Low Borrow Bridge, known as Castlehows, is very remote from centres of population and was difficult of access until the building of the railway; so it remained unvisited and unrecognised by earlier antiquaries. Indeed its true character was not known until the early nineteenth century. On the fort-platform itself a regular cattle-fair took place in Victorian times and probably earlier still, perhaps because it lay upon a drove-road. No doubt the Roman roads still leading to it and the convenient enclosure of the fort in an area where there was little enclosure at that date promoted its use as a fair-site; the present farm house was once an inn, which was no doubt a further inducement. We may wonder, however, which came first, fair or inn. This once-remote valley now echoes to the roar of traffic on the main west-coast railway line and the M6 motorway.

At Burrow part of the site – not that of the fort but rather of its civil settlement – was occupied by a medieval hamlet. In the 1640s Col. Briggs built his house here, known in a deed of 1649 as 'the Hall lately erected in Overburrow',[5] which was in turn rebuilt and extended by Robert Fenwick in about 1740. The present Georgian mansion and stables lie at the edge of the fort and parallel to its east wall. This can hardly be coincidental. Perhaps more was visible of the fort platform at that time, influencing the position of the Hall. The fact that the grounds of Burrow Hall are emparked has protected the remains from disturbance of an agricultural nature and despite all the building work of the eighteenth century it was not until as late as 1952 that the exact site of the fort was established.

Lancaster's civilian settlement, or at least its eastern part, is the direct ancestor of the present town, which has been recognisably urban in character since at least 1193, when its first borough charter was given. The fort itself lies partly under the Priory church and partly under the medieval Castle. The northern slopes of the ridge on which the fort stood have been protected from agriculture and development in medieval and later times by the fact that in 1094 the whole area of what are now known as 'the Vicarage Fields' became the property of Lancaster Priory and, after the dissolution of the Priory,[6] glebeland belonging to the Vicar. In 1949 this land was purchased by Lancaster City Council, which allowed a series of excavations to take place there. Other parts of the fort are by no means as accessible and it was not until results of various excavations of the 1970s were synthesised that even the broad outlines of the fort could be established with any confidence.

Beyond the forts and their civilian settlements were the farmsteads which supplied most of their food needs as well as providing a subsistence for the bulk of the native British population. In the absence of archaeological excavation we can say little at present of a detailed character about these farmsteads, though the locations of

4. The Vale of Lonsdale engraved 1831 by W. Le Petit after J. Henderson. This viewpoint, above Crook O'Lune, looking towards Ingleborough (the prominent flat topped hill), was very popular with artists. Georgian tourists came this way because of scenic qualities but gained an added frisson from the presence of Roman remains. (Lancaster City Museums.)

many are known, particularly in the upper Lune valley, and quite a few survive as earthworks. Ironically, these may represent the failures while the successful ones lie under modern farmsteads, their sites long determined by the availability of water and pasture.

Supplies of coal, building stone, iron ore and clay for bricks, tiles and pottery were all available locally and were exploited during the Roman period, probably under military supervision. The wilder fells no doubt sheltered wild animals which Roman officers hunted for sport but which also provided an important reservoir of protein for the native population, especially in winter. Likewise the Lune estuary, the coastal marshes and Morecambe Bay will have teemed with fish such as salmon and sea-trout as well as shrimps, flounders and shell-fish, and also with a wide variety of wildfowl. One would expect farmsteads in this coastal area to have had a dual economy based upon agriculture and fishing/gathering.

Notes to Chapter 1

1. Swain, 1992, 8–12
2. Rivet and Smith, 1979, 382; Ekwall, 1947, 293
3. Park, 1990, 122–4
4. Shotter and White, 1990, 32–40
5. Chippendall, 1933, 98
6. White, 1993, 35

Chapter 2

Roman Conquest and Occupation

THROUGHOUT the period of the Roman occupation, the Lune valley clearly constituted an important route of communication through the frontier-hinterland. However, as we have seen, our knowledge of different parts of it and of different sites within it remains very uneven. There is, therefore, a danger that we may generalise from what we do know, and assume that the generalisations can be made to apply more widely. This is certainly true of the questions of conquest and occupation.

In recent years, a number of studies have tried to establish the pattern of conquest and consolidation by the Romans in what had been the territory of the Brigantes.[1] Soon after the arrival in Britain of the conquering army in A.D. 43, it appears that a treaty was established with Cartimandua, queen of the Brigantes. The intention behind this treaty was to leave Rome free to pursue the conquest of the south, the midlands and Wales without having to fear too much from the northern tribe. Cartimandua, in her turn, gained a degree of security of tenure with respect to factional rivals within the tribe, the most serious of whom was Venutius, to whom she was married.[2]

This arrangement broadly achieved stability in northern England until *c.*A.D. 70, although uncertainties in the relationship of Venutius and Cartimandua called for Roman vigilance and, on a few occasions apparently, a need for military intervention. It is possible that Cartimandua's main sphere of influence lay to the east of the Pennines – perhaps in the vicinity of the later legionary fortress at York or at Stanwick; her husband's ability, however, to call upon aid from outside the tribal territory suggests a proximity to Wales, and thus a principal sphere of influence to the west of the Pennines.

The distribution of hill-forts further suggests the possibility of localised, quasi-independent, hegemonies; the Setantii, whose harbour (*portus*) is mentioned by Ptolemy, and the Carvetii, recorded on an inscription at Brougham, may have been two of these.[3] Although the political geography of Brigantian territory can now hardly be reconstructed, it is a reasonable suggestion that major rivers played a part in the division of tribal territory and, of course, were also responsible for the fertility of soils which must have

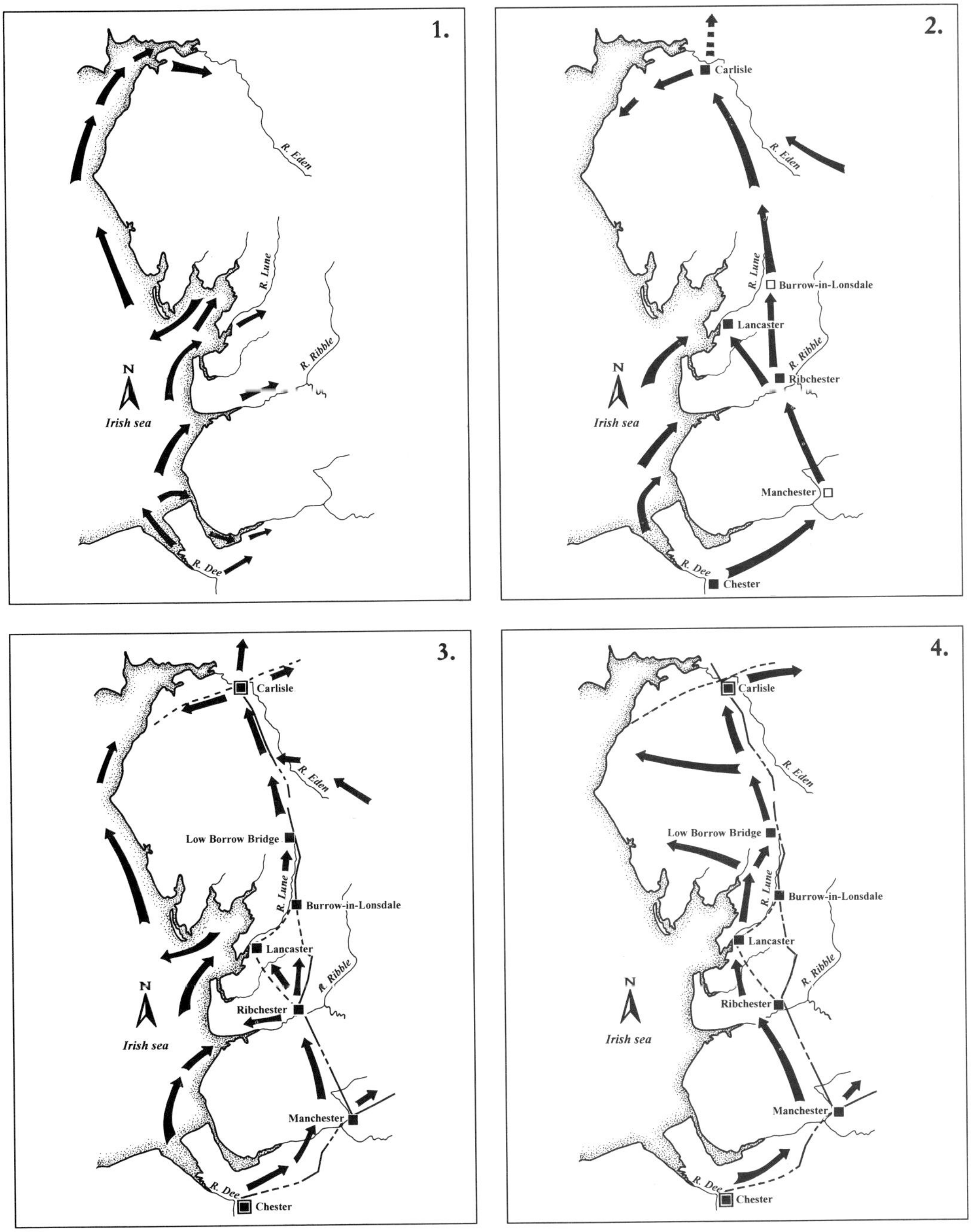

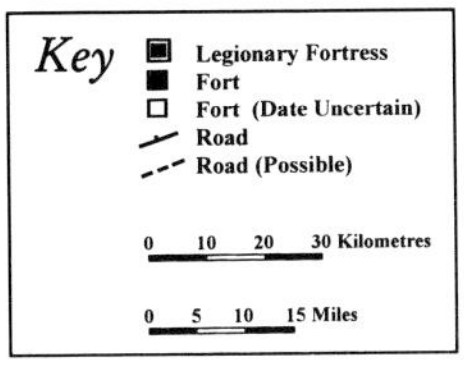

5. Maps to illustrate Roman campaigns:
(1) before A.D. 69;
(2) by Cerialis (A.D. 72);
(3) by Agricola (A.D. 78); and
(4) between A.D. 90 and 120, as they affected the north-west.
(P. Thompson/W. Moore after P. Lee.)

constituted a major source of prosperity and an object of political and economic rivalry.

Our evidence concerning Roman intervention into western Brigantia is based partly on deductions from artefactual evidence and partly on rather vague statements to be found in Roman writers. It is clear that the 50s and 60s saw a slow Roman extension into the southern Pennines as far north as Chester, which was as significant for the conquest of Wales as it was for that of north-west England. Although detail is lacking, it seems that military intervention into Lancashire and Cumbria had also to be organised during this period. Such intervention appears to have been achieved with troops transported by coastal shipping from the Dee and disembarked at suitable points of access. The river-estuaries provided such access, and it is more than likely that one of these estuaries was the Lune. It is not clear how deeply inland such intervention penetrated; although apparently no permanent troop-dispositions resulted, the action must have been sufficiently effective to destroy cohesion amongst groups of tribesmen. 'Structural' evidence for such activity, therefore, is likely to come in the form of marching-camps rather than forts. Such sites will on low ground, subject to generations of ploughing, prove to be particularly difficult to locate, and, even if located, extremely hard to date.

The factional rivalry amongst the Brigantes came to a head in A.D. 69,[4] a year in which Roman armies were distracted by partisanship in their own civil war. Venutius appears finally to have outwitted Cartimandua, who had to be rescued by Roman troops; as a consequence of her departure the Brigantes were transformed into a hostile tribe. Vespasian, the eventual victor in the civil war, had to look to Britain with some urgency, and sent his son-in-law, the highly-experienced Petillius Cerialis, to the province as governor (A.D. 71–74). Cerialis' movements are not known in detail, though it is generally assumed that he advanced from Lincoln to York, and thence perhaps to Corbridge and across Stainmore to Carlisle. Under Cerialis, the commander of the Twentieth Legion – (based at Wroxeter, but soon to be transferred to Chester) – was the future governor, Gnaeus Julius Agricola. It is evident [5] that he was given a considerable amount of independent responsibility, presumably to act west of the Pennines.

On this occasion, Brigantian territory appears to have been approached by sea as well as overland; thus, the Lune estuary was probably penetrated again, and on this occasion contact made with troops who had advanced by land from Chester; dating by dendrochronology of timbers recovered from the rampart-corduroy (base) at Ribchester suggests an initial construction-date for the first phase of the fort no later than the period of Cerialis' governorship. The fact that similar dating-evidence has come from rampart-timbers at Carlisle makes it highly likely that troops disembarked in the neighbourhood of Lancaster, followed the Lune to meet up with

6. Aerial photograph of the Roman marching-camp at Rey Cross on Stainmore, perhaps a relic from the campaigns of Cerialis. Such marching-camps show up best on wild and marginal land. Their counterparts on better soils have often been ploughed away. There must be many which have disappeared without trace. (Photograph courtesy of G. D. B. Jones/Manunair.)

colleagues near Burrow-in-Lonsdale, and then marched together up the Lune and Eden valleys to Carlisle, effecting a rendezvous near Brougham with those troops whom Cerialis had himself led across Stainmore. At present, evidence west of the Pennines of permanent forts of the early 70s is limited to Ribchester and Carlisle, and Blennerhasset in north-west Cumbria.[6] It seems likely, however, that others were established, presumably close to later permanent sites, if not actually on the same sites. Significantly, penetration of the Lune and Eden valleys, and of the Solway Plain, will have assured Roman control of the best agricultural land in the north-west.

These military activities, crowned by the defeat of Venutius, probably at Stanwick in north Yorkshire, appear to have destroyed the cohesion of the Brigantes, since through the mid-70s attention switched afresh to Wales. It was not until Agricola returned to Britain in A.D. 77, now as governor, that the Brigantes again became the subject of military activity. In Agricola's second campaign (in A.D. 78), he seems to have completed the conversion of the fort at Chester into a legionary fortress, and to have swept northwards through Brigantian territory, again heading apparently for Carlisle and Corbridge, and formalising a link between them by way of the road known since medieval times as 'the Stanegate'.

It is evident that Agricola was able to rely on the mutual suspicion of groups amongst the Brigantes in order to profit by a policy of 'divide and rule'. Once again, it appears that the overland route was followed from Chester (via Northwich, Manchester and Ribchester) to Burrow-in-Lonsdale, Low Borrow Bridge, and on to Brougham and Carlisle. It is clear that this route was linked to the coast along the Ribble and along the Lune; although doubts persist over the dating of Burrow-in-Lonsdale and Low Borrow Bridge, there is no doubt that a turf-and-clay rampart, located during excavations at Lancaster in three different places in 1971, 1973 and 1975, is at least as early as Agricola's governorship.[7]

The remainder of Agricola's period of office was spent in the conquest of Scotland, and Brigantian territory west of the Lune and the Eden was left largely untouched. Agricola's recall in A.D. 83 was soon followed by a change of policy in Britain; in order to cope with new and dangerous pressures in central Europe, one of Britain's four legions was removed. A garrison consisting now of three legions could not hold the whole of Britain; Scotland was consequently relinquished.

The implication of Agricola's son-in-law, the historian Tacitus, that this represented a timid sell-out in Britain, is called into question by the fact, established beyond doubt in the archaeological record, that the retreat from Scotland was accompanied by a vigorous consolidation of Brigantian territory. Over a period from the late 80s to the early 120s, the Lake District was brought within the policing-network of the Roman army, and a new northward link was forged up the Lancashire coastal plain, providing Lancaster with a direct north/south route of communication, and probably at this stage one across the sands of Morecambe Bay to south-west Cumbria.[8] A parallel element to this new construction was the consolidation of existing sites, by rebuilding them in stone; an inscription from Lancaster (as also from Chester and York) dates this work to the reign of Trajan (A.D. 98–117).[9]

This period also saw continued pressure on the northern frontier region: a frontier-line was established along the Stanegate road between Corbridge and Carlisle with a series of large forts (such as Vindolanda) and watchtowers: the Stanegate was also extended westwards to the coast at Kirkbride.[10] Again, however, we are poorly served for detail. Trajan's reign was dominated first by his war in Dacia and then by campaigns to facilitate his extremely ambitious plans in the east. Whether or not this necessitated further troop-withdrawals in Britain is not clear, though it is evident that, by the time of Hadrian's accession in A.D. 117, the situation in Britain had deteriorated to the point where Hadrian's biographer could observe that when Hadrian became emperor 'the Britons could no longer be held under Roman control'.[11]

The precise location of the trouble is not clear, although its seriousness is demonstrated by the fact that victories needed to be secured (and commemorated on the coinage) before Hadrian came to Britain himself in A.D. 122 to institute a new policy – the strengthening (and eventual replacement) of the Stanegate-frontier by Hadrian's Wall. This not only separated Romans from barbarians, but also offered the opportunity for consolidation and the development of prosperity behind a clear frontier-zone.

How much (if any) trouble had occurred to the south of the line of Hadrian's Wall is unclear, though a group of Trajanic/early Hadrianic coin-hoards from Lancashire may provide an indication of unsettled conditions.[12] However, that there was not general uncertainty in Brigantian territory is clear from the fact that at least at one important fort – Ribchester – the surrounding area could be considered sufficiently secure for its garrison of Asturian cavalry to be put into a forward position on the Wall itself. Our lack of information about fort-garrisons, however, prevents us from pursuing further a line of investigation which would clearly help in establishing the political temperature of Brigantian territory in the first half of the second century A.D.. That the lower end of the Lune valley was witnessing the establishment of settled conditions in the 120s would appear to be an implication of the fine Hadrianic milestone from Caton, explicitly dated to Hadrian's middle years.[13]

In contrast to the aggressive Trajan, Hadrian was a consolidator, looking to firm and clear frontiers with a steady development of Romanised prosperity behind them; warfare was necessary only to secure such conditions. How far Antoninus Pius' renewed attention to southern Scotland, which culminated in the building of the Antonine Wall in A.D. 142, was conceived in that light is hard to say. It is, however, clear that a reference in the Greek writer, Pausanias, often taken to indicate renewed disturbance amongst the Brigantes, cannot be used to press that case.[14] Whatever the reasons for the Antonine advance into Scotland, it certainly meant redeployment of troops from elsewhere, and it appears that Lancaster lost its garrison during this period.

The occupation of the Antonine Wall came to an end in *c.*A.D. 163, but conditions in the north-west evidently remained unsettled; some have argued the incidence of coin-hoards [15] as evidence of this, and references in classical authors certainly indicate that during the second half of the second century A.D., Roman armies were involved in hostilities in the north. Further, a tombstone of Flavius Romanus from Ambleside, dating probably to the early third century,[16] reveals with unusual frankness that this soldier was killed by the enemy *inside his fort*. On the other hand, evidence from non-military sites points to the second century as a period of growing prosperity and Romanisation; those Brigantes living east of the Pennines received a measure of local control over their affairs with the establishment of an administrative centre at Aldborough (*Isurium Brigantum*).

Although many now view with scepticism the notion that Hadrian's Wall and the north were overwhelmed by barbarian armies in A.D. 197, the incidence of building and rebuilding-inscriptions [17] in the area suggests a prolonged period of localised difficulties. That all was not well, however, is amply demonstrated by Septimius Severus' decision in the first decade of the third century temporarily to move his court to York, and use it as a base for renewed military campaigning in Scotland – perhaps intending not so much to incorporate Scotland into the province as to emasculate Scottish fighting-power for a generation at least to buy time for calmer and more prosperous conditions to establish themselves further south.

Success in this was eventually achieved by his elder son and successor, Caracalla, although the use of financial subsidies did not please those contemporary commentators who preferred clear military victories. The success of Caracalla was, however, tangible; trade evidently opened up between the province and southern Scotland, and it seems that some at least of the forts of Hadrian's Wall could be left ungarrisoned. A further indication of the development of peace and prosperity in the north-west is to be seen in the establishment, around the middle of the third century A.D., of a further area of local self-government amongst the Brigantes in the form of the *Civitas Carvetiorum*.[18] Although little information survives on the tribal territory concerned, it seems that the administrative centre was at Carlisle, and that the ability of the tribal aristocracy to maintain the local-government function was probably based on the prosperity resulting from agricultural exploitation of areas such as the Solway Plain, and the Eden and Upper Lune valleys.

On the other hand, the *general* sense of prosperity and well-being within the empire had been diminishing since the mid-second century A.D.. The new dominance in politics given by Septimius Severus to the army was the direct cause of the anarchy that threatened to split the empire apart, and which led to two secessionist movements which involved Britain – the independent Empire of the Gauls (A.D. 259–273) and the rebellion of Carausius and Allectus (A.D. 287–296). The anarchy also exacerbated inflationary tendencies in the empire's economy which developed into such chaotic conditions by the middle of the third century that the coinage appears to have become virtually worthless and grossly inadequate coin-supplies had to be topped up with locally-manufactured pieces, often of execrable quality. The coherence of the empire's trade clearly suffered as a result, bringing with it an inevitably greater emphasis on local self-sufficiency.

To many it must have seemed that the Roman empire was in terminal decline; that it was not was due largely to the vigorous policies of Diocletian and Constantine (A.D. 284–337), who tried to repair the damage done to the military integrity of the empire as well as to its political and economic fabric. To this effort and its effect upon Britain we shall return in a later chapter.

Notes to Chapter 2

1. Potter, 1979, 351–367; Shotter, 1980 and 1994.
2. Tacitus, *Histories* III. 45 and *Annals* XII. 40.
3. Ptolemy, *Geographia*, II. 3 (Setantii); *JRS* LV (1965), 224 (Carvetii). See Higham, 1986, 147.
4. Shotter, 1993, 7–29.
5. Tacitus, *Life of Agricola* 8.
6. Evans and Scull, 1990.
7. Jones and Shotter, 1988, 26–58.
8. Shotter, 1995.
9. *RIB* 604; cf *RIB* 464 (Chester) and 665–666 (York).
10. Jones, 1982.
11. Spartianus in *Writers of the Augustan History*, Life of Hadrian 5. 2.
12. Shotter, 1978.
13. *RIB* 2272.
14. Pausanias, *Description of Greece* VIII, 43; for a discussion, see Hind, 1977.
15. Shotter, 1990, 211; also Breeze, 1975.
16. *JRS* LIII (1963), 160.
17. Potter, 1979, 358–63.
18. *JRS* LV (1965), 224 (Brougham) and *RIB* 933 (Old Penrith); see Higham and Jones, 1985.

Chapter 3

Lancaster

DESPITE the imposing nature of the Castle and the Priory Church, Lancaster's development in medieval times was relatively slow; Scottish attacks and epidemics ensured that it remained a modest town until the eighteenth century, when the development of the port and its trading across the Atlantic led to a new prosperity, which was amongst other things translated into building. The fact that Lancaster has little to show for the medieval period and that its oldest buildings are predominantly Georgian is a consequence of this 'arrested development'.[1]

Many of the major finds of Roman material in Lancaster came to light during the period of expansion in the eighteenth century and later in the following century when major services, such as sewers and railways, were under construction. Nonetheless, references to ancient structures and Roman finds go back well beyond that; Leland, Camden and many others [2] reported walls on Castle Hill and in the area of Church Street, but these reports were dominated by speculation on the significance of the Wery Wall – speculation which persisted until the questions about it were finally resolved in the excavations of 1973. The Wery Wall – the name means no more than 'Defensive' Wall – has dominated the thinking of historians and archaeologists, although it represents only a small part (albeit of importance) of Lancaster's Roman history.

Historians of Lancaster are fortunate in that the record of much that was found was ably kept by such men as Father Thomas West (in his *Guide to the Lakes*, published in 1778) and Edward Baines (in his *History of the County Palatine of Lancaster*, published in 1824); further, lists of material which had been found were collated and published by W. Thompson Watkin (in his *Roman Lancashire* of 1883). These and other less well-known antiquarians ensured that a great deal of what was uncovered was not lost, and published their observations made at times when the townscape presented an appearance very different from that which exists to-day.[3] A more detailed, but no less significant example of this kind of service is provided by the recording by Thomas Dalzell and Corbyn Barrow of Roman coins found in the nineteenth century. Their notebooks, meticulously kept, are preserved in Lancaster City Museum, and have enabled provenances to be attached to many coins in the Museum's collection. Some of the sites reported by such writers as

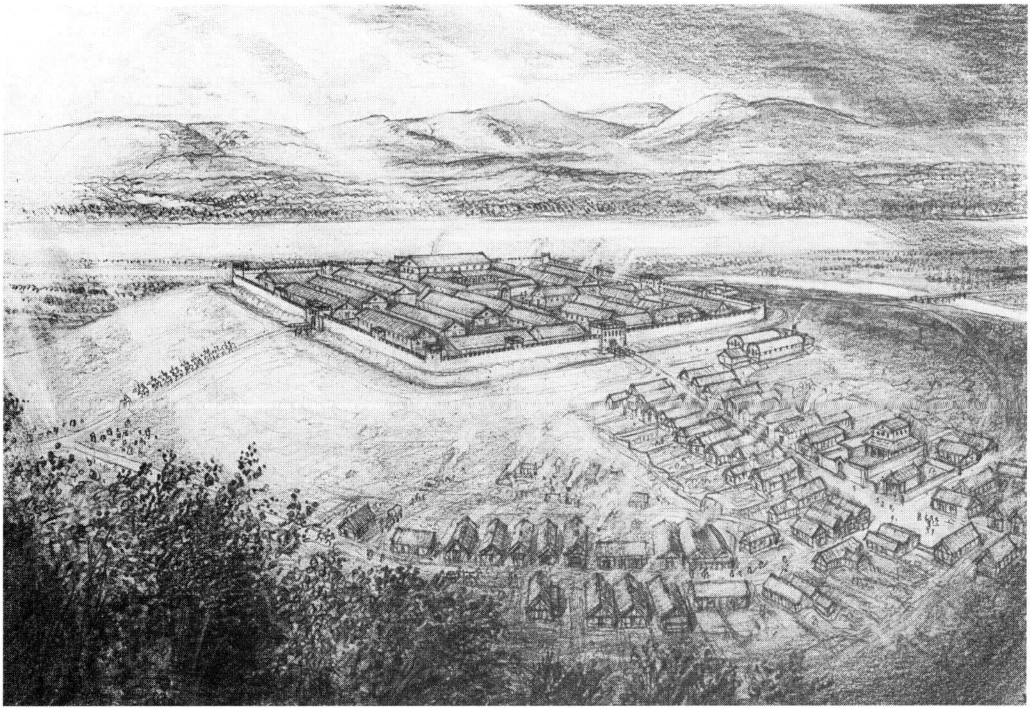

7. A reconstruction by David Vale of the Roman fort and civil settlement of Lancaster in the second century A.D., as it might have appeared from high ground to the south-east.

these have been 'tested' by intermittent excavations, conducted on a wide variety of scales in the present century.[4]

As a consequence, we are often able to put antiquarian reports alongside the results of excavations, and arrive at plausible accounts of aspects and parts at least of Lancaster's history as a Roman fort and civilian settlement (*vicus*). Of course, there are still many gaps, both physical and chronological, in our understanding, and the non-availability to excavation of crucial areas, such as are covered by the Castle and the Priory Church, is likely to leave a number of our questions unanswered for a considerable time to come.

It has long been assumed that the earliest, permanent, occupation of the fort-site on Castle Hill occurred during the governorship of Agricola, presumably during the course of his second campaign (A.D. 78). Tacitus' reference in his account of that campaign to the Roman army's operations in an area of 'estuaries and woods' seems appropriate to Lancaster and its hinterland.[5] Roman forts of Agricola's time were generally square or rectangular, with ramparts of clay or clay-and-turf. The external face of the rampart would have been battered and the inside often revetted with vertical timbers. Outside there would have been one or more 'V'-shaped ditches, and perhaps timber palisades also, whilst inside a metalled service-road (the *intervallum*-road) ran all the way round the fort's perimeter. The buildings would have been constructed of timber, and the ramparts

8. A section through the rampart of the Agricolan fort at the Old Vicarage, Lancaster in 1975 showing the interleaving of humus and clay from the original turf and, at the very bottom, traces of a fascine drain, made from silver birch twigs.

pierced with at least four timber gate-and-guardtower complexes.[6] Elements of such structures have been identified in at least four excavations on Castle Hill, including a very fine rampart-section adjacent to the Old Vicarage; the excavations have in fact located elements of the defences on all sides of the hill, with the exception of the south. Further, these defences appear to have had two phases of activity followed by a period (probably short) of abandonment. It has been assumed that the second phase, which represented an enlargement of the first fort, was constructed in the 80s, perhaps following the general withdrawal from Scotland in *c.*A.D. 87.

It is, however, worth considering alternative models: the presence in the recorded coin-sample of pre-Flavian *aes* (copper/bronze) coins is suggestive of the possibility of activity at Lancaster prior to Agricola's governorship; indeed, within that group of coins the fact that a number are earlier than Nero's reign may point to military operations at this point of the Lancashire coast as early as the 60s A.D.. A context for such activity is provided by the deteriorating stability of Brigantian politics at the time.[7] If the Lancaster-area was included at so early a date, the likely *structural* evidence for it would be found in the form of a campaign-camp rather than a permanent fort. In view of the fact that it is now regarded as certain that Carlisle and Ribchester were established as permanent forts during the governorship of Petillius Cerialis (A.D. 71–4), it is not inconceivable that the two Flavian phases recognised at Lancaster belong to Cerialis and Agricola, and are followed by a period of abandonment from the late 80s into the middle or late 90s.

The northern rampart of the primary fort was 9 feet wide, and, despite great vertical compression, still stood to a height of 5 feet with a very clearly battered outer face; it was constructed of clay-

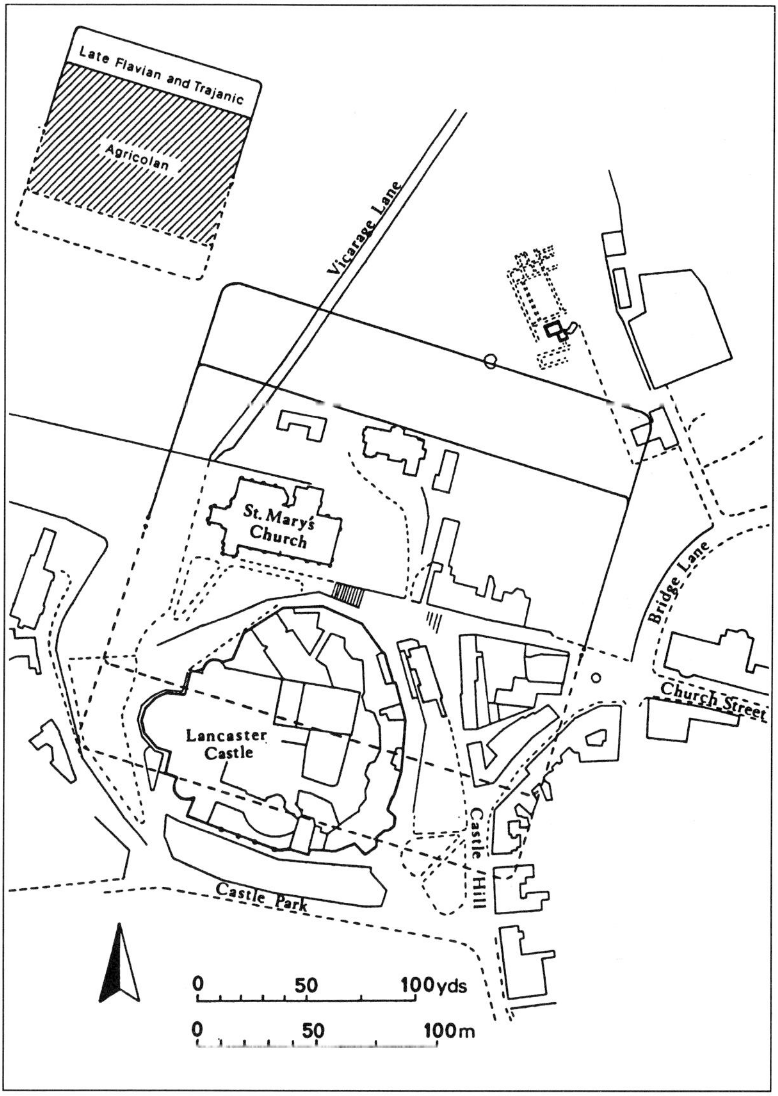

9. Plan of the successive Roman forts at Lancaster. (P. Lee.)

and-turf, on a brushwood-foundation. Elsewhere, evidence was found of a timber guard-tower at the north-east corner, and elements of the eastern gateway, so positioned as to indicate the Roman origin of Church Street. Outside this eastern gate, there were two ditches with evidence of a palisade of timber stakes on the inner lip of the second ditch; these ditches appeared to be curving inwards through 90 degrees, as if to accommodate the fort's exit-road. The only evidence of internal buildings was of two phases of timber-structures (probably barracks) near to the Old Vicarage; these had evidently been destroyed by fire.

The dimensions of this fort would appear to have been approximately 615 feet (east to west) by approximately 400 feet (north to south), although the latter dimension must remain conjectural since the southern side of the fort has never been revealed and presumably lies beneath the Castle. Such dimensions would argue for a fort with an area of approximately 5. 6 acres, which puts it on the large side, but comparable with Ribchester.

The second Flavian phase involved enlargement by pushing the northern rampart northwards by about 120 feet; if this was matched on the southern side, the fort's eastern and western ramparts would have been extended to around 650 feet in length, producing a fort which, at over 9 acres, was large for the period. Further, the general shape will thereby have been changed from rectangular to nearly square. If, in the primary phase, the main gateway lay on the eastern side, it is possible that in the secondary phase the fort was re-orientated through 90 degrees, moving the main gateway to the north, although this *may* have happened later.

We have evidence at various periods of cavalry-units being based at Lancaster; the *Ala Augusta* and the *Ala Sebosiana* are cited on inscriptions,[8] and near the east gateway a timber-lined well had been filled with stable-refuse. Certainly, the primary phase of the fort was sufficiently large to house a five-hundred-strong cavalry-unit, whilst the enlarged fort may have been garrisoned by a one-thousand-strong cavalry unit, or by a smaller unit in association with a detachment, perhaps of legionary troops. At any rate, the size of the fort is a clear indication of its significance in the policing-network established in north-west England.

Early in the second century,[9] after reoccupation the fort was further refurbished – on this occasion by adding a stone-wall to the face of the secondary clay-and-turf rampart, and probably by replacing some at least of the internal buildings in stone. It is probably significant that some of the timbers which were recovered from the timber-lined well situated near the east gate of the fort represented re-used building material. Little is known of this fort, although the medieval rampart-system visible in the western Vicarage Field is known to overlie precisely the north-west corner of the defences of the Trajanic fort.

Coin-evidence suggests that the fort may have lost at least part of its garrison with the renewed push into Scotland ordered by Antoninus Pius in A.D. 142. Although the Antonine Wall was abandoned by the mid-160s and troops presumably returned to Hadrian's Wall and northern England, it is unclear what happened at Lancaster: structural and artefactual evidence do not present a coherent picture. However, in view of the fact that the *vicus* continued to thrive through the later second century, it might be suggested that, after the Antonine occupation of Scotland, the large fort at Lancaster did not receive back a *full* garrison; occupation by a unit of *normal* size – that is, five hundred men – might be expected to have left areas of

10. A timber-lined well, found near the east gate in 1973. The timbers had been re-used from earlier buildings and the well contained quantities of stable-sweepings. These have been analysed to show what the horses ate and what bedding they were given.

the fort apparently unoccupied. It will not be possible to resolve such dilemmas until more is known of the southern end of the fort, and an opportunity arises to study a substantial area of the fort's interior. A further point of consideration is that the large courtyard-building, parts of which have been excavated in the northern Vicarage Field (see below on p. 27f.), would appear to have obtruded upon the northern defences of the fort.

In the middle of the third century A.D. we have clear evidence of occupation in the form of an inscription [10] commemorating the rebuilding from ground-level of a bath-house and basilica which had 'collapsed through old age'. The bath-house is almost certainly that which stood immediately outside the eastern rampart of the fort, whilst the basilica is best understood as a *basilica equestris exercitatoria,* a special drill-hall attached to the headquarters-buildings of cavalry-forts. If these important buildings had in fact collapsed through old age, this might suggest that the rebuilding followed a period of neglect, presumably because of demilitarisation. On the other hand, such a formula might represent a euphemism to cover violent destruction. At any rate, reconstruction was carried out by the *Ala Sebosiana,* a cavalry-unit, whose name figures on a lead-sealing from the western Vicarage field, and also on a lead-sealing found at Brough-under-Stainmore and on a writing-tablet from Carlisle.[11]

It has already been suggested that Lancaster's size argues for the fort of considerable local (or regional) importance, and that its garrison may at one time have been partly legionary; this suggestion receives some support from the fact that the collection of stamped roofing-tiles[12] from Lancaster itself and its associated tilery at Quernmore includes one fragment from Lancaster with a possible legionary origin. Further, a dedication survives which was made to

11. A bronze diploma found at Malpas, Cheshire, which lists among other units the Ala Sebosiana. Such diplomas were presented to soldiers on their retirement, to be used as evidence of their Roman citizenship. (CIL XVI.48, photograph by permission of Trustees of the British Museum.)

the Romano-Celtic god, Mars Cocidius, by a high-ranking official, Lucius Vibenius, who is described as the governor's aide (*beneficiarius consularis*).[13] It is possible that the large courtyard-building identified in the northern Vicarage field was his official residence.

Major changes were made to the fort in the fourth century;

around A.D. 340, a completely new fort was constructed, of which the Wery Wall was a part. This fort was built on a new alignment and destroyed buildings which stood in its way, such as the bath-house of the courtyard building. As stated above, the Wery Wall itself appears to represent the core of an external bastion (or artillery-mounting) which stood at the north angle of this fort. Other possible elements of this fort have been located over the years, which suggest a structure which was sub-rectangular, enclosing an area in excess of 5.5 acres, and possibly as large as 9 acres, and was possibly aligned to the contemporary course of the river. The fact that this structure was characterised by thick, heavy – and presumably, high – stone walls suggests a parallel with sites on the west coast such as Cardiff, Caernarfon and Caer Gybi, and with the series of 'Saxon-Shore' forts in the south-east.

This apparent attention to coastal defence fits well with the changing military imperatives of Roman Britain in the fourth century; it should also be noted that the discovery on Cockersands Moss of two statuettes to the Irish god, Nodens (or Nodons), strengthens Lancaster's maritime connections in the fourth century;[14] for a new temple to this god was constructed at Lydney, on the Severn estuary, *after* A.D. 360, and contains a mosaic which possibly carries the title of the commander of what survived of the British fleet (*Classis Britannica*). The Lancaster-area has also produced an inscription[15] which contains the name of a unit with clear maritime connections – a unit of boatmen (*Numerus Barcariorum*). Such soldiers may have, amongst other things, acted as lightermen, unloading deep-draughted vessels in Morecambe Bay, and bringing their cargoes into port at Lancaster. This inscription, which was found at Halton-on-Lune, is not specifically dated, but may indicate a unit in garrison at the new fort at Lancaster in the fourth century with skills suitable to a coastal site and which equipped it to handle the type of threat which was emerging in the fourth century. There are considerable problems on epigraphic grounds, however, in accepting this inscription as anything like as late as the fourth century.

No internal buildings of this new fort have been recognised, and it is possible, although not certain, that it housed both soldiers and civilians, since recent excavations in the *vicus* have indicated an abandonment of properties there around A.D. 340, presumably as the security-situation in the north-west became more tenuous. Certainly, disruption was caused in the 340s and 350s by the feuding between the sons of Constantine and the emergence in the west of the rebel-emperor, Magnentius. This was followed shortly afterwards by the so-called 'conspiracy of the barbarians' in A.D. 367 which inflicted much damage to military sites in the north, but which was followed by reconstruction which appears to have enhanced the importance of coastal sites such as Ravenglass, Maryport and Bowness-on-Solway. That occupation of the Wery-Wall fort continued until late in the fourth and probably into the fifth century is clear from the evidence both of pottery and coins. In common with other sites in the north, it is likely that, by the early fifth century, the occupants of the fort exercised a purely local function of supplying and defending themselves, and might be best described as a local citizen-militia.

Most Roman forts supported extra-mural civilian settlement, since the presence of a garrison of well-paid troops represented a market which had needs which others could supply for profit. In the case of Lancaster, the vibrancy of such a settlement will have been enormously enhanced by the additional role of a port. Although there may have been extra-mural settlement all around the fort, it is likely to have been most concentrated to the east and north-east of the fort, between Church Street and the river. Although no reports of harbour-facilities by the riverside have ever been confirmed, it seems inconceivable that they did not exist.

It is likely that the civilian-settlements enjoyed different levels of status, and certainly grew to different sizes, depending presumably on their commercial success. It is, however, becoming increasingly clear that it is dangerous to generalise about them, although this inevitably happens since so few have been substantially investigated.[16]

Excavations and aerial photography appear to indicate that such settlements were not planned, but grew in an informal way as need and opportunity dictated. It is likely that, since they fell under the general jurisdiction of the fort-commander, most did not have a civilian administration and therefore lacked the buildings that went with such a role. Buildings usually in evidence are a bath-house, a hotel (*mansio*), temples to accommodate a wide variety of official and unofficial religious cults, bars and brothels. The most common structures, however, were the long, narrow, strip-buildings, situated with their gable-ends fronting the streets; some of these might have provided living-accommodation for soldiers' families, whilst others might be better described as business-premises, consisting of a shop on the street-frontage, with living-accommodation behind it, and perhaps, at the rear, a yard where the owners/tenants could make or process what was sold in the shop; such arrangements represented a Mediterranean importation. It is possible by analogy with other sites that areas of these settlements were devoted to particular activities. We might expect that many would be involved in the food-trade, or in manufacturing objects in cloth, leather, terra-cotta, or metal.

In the case of Lancaster, existing evidence suggests that the settlement centred on present-day Church Street, the exit-road from the fort's east gate. However, there is also evidence of settlement on the north and west flanks of the fort. Evidently, the most significant building so far located is situated on Castle Hill itself immediately outside the postulated position of the fort's north gate. It appears to have been a large courtyard-building with a bath-suite at the southern end. The hey-day of this building seems to have been in the later

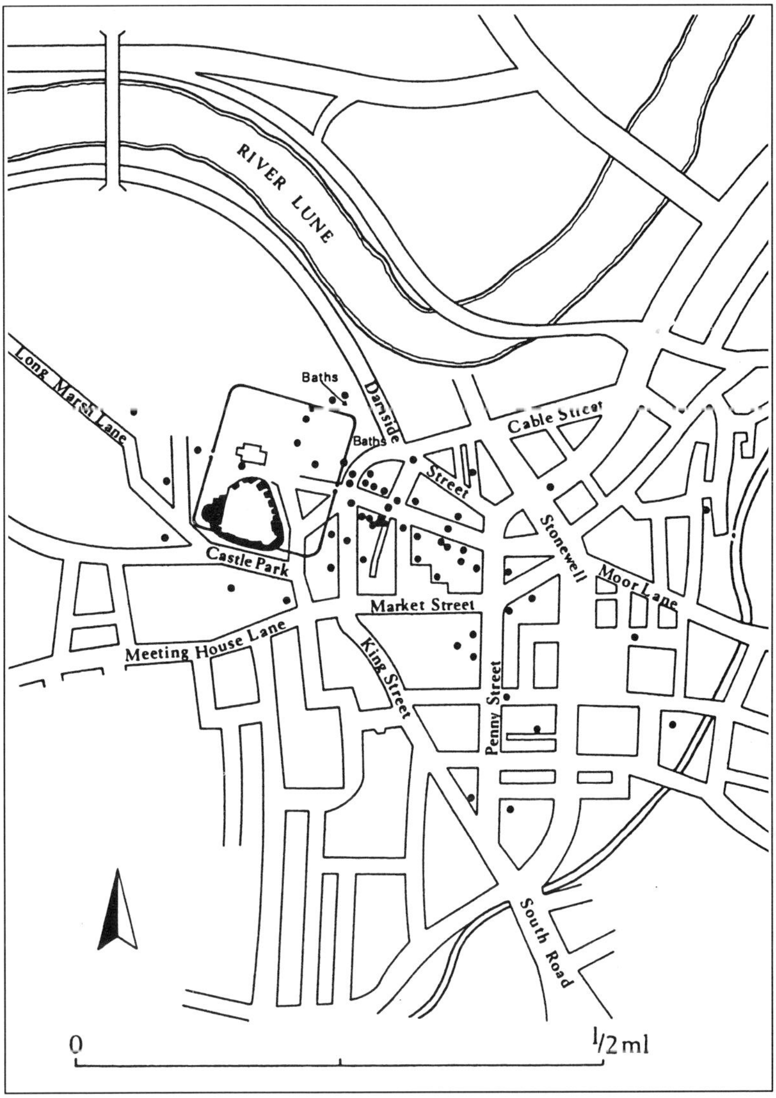

12. Plan of Lancaster showing the fort and related civilian settlement. The latter is at present best defined by the distribution of Roman finds, but excavation may show that this is an over-simplified view. (P. Lee.)

second and third centuries and it was destroyed by the construction of the Wery-Wall fort in or around A.D. 340.[17] It was evidently a building of some consequence, not only because it had its own bath-suite, but also because of the amount of painted wall-plaster found amongst its debris.[18] Although its overall dimensions are difficult to recover, it appears to have occupied a space of approximately 180 feet by 80 feet. The obvious interpretations of this building are *either* that it was a *mansio* (hotel for official travellers) *or* that it was the residence of an important official, such as a regional centurion (*centurio regionarius*) or a governor's aide (*beneficiarius consularis*).[19]

13. The bath-suite of the courtyard building in Vicarage Field, during excavation in 1973, showing the stone pilae which supported the floor and the great V-shaped ditch cut through it in the fourth century A.D.

The fort's bath-house was located just outside the eastern rampart, and is now encased in concrete beneath the office-block known as Mitre House. The bath-house was studied under very unfavourable conditions in 1973–4, and any conclusions are tentative: however, one area produced a substantial hypocaust, constructed probably in the second century. The floor-supports were provided by *pilae* of square tiles, although these had been supplemented by roughly-hewn stone *pilae*, presumably to halt sagging to the floor. It is not impossible that these represent the repairs alluded to in the third-century bath-house inscription.[20] A further building contained architectural debris of a type that suggested that it might have been of the *basilica*-type.

Other buildings in the civilian settlement have been recorded or viewed at various times in fragmentary form along Church Street, China Street, Cheapside and Penny Street,[21] although considerable damage has been done to archaeological deposits on the street-frontages by cellar-digging. Little substantial information has emerged to indicate the purposes of buildings, although most appear to have been of the strip-building type, constructed in timber or stone-and-timber and separated by 'ditches' or alley-ways ('lanes'), some of which have modern 'successors' which still run between Church Street and Market Street. There is an indication of a possible temple-site on the southern side of Church Street, and adjacent to a

14. Detail of the bath-suite showing stone pilae and the slots in the wall which originally held flue-tiles to conduct heat up through the superstructure.

site excavated in 1988 and 1992, which itself produced fragments of a pottery-mask, possibly of Dionysiac type; a pillar-base from the Masonic Hall, found in 1958, offers a clue to another substantial building. Although buildings have individual chronologies, an overall date for the civilian settlement appears to run from the late-first century A.D. to the mid-fourth.

It is possible, too, that there was a temple of the Persian god, Mithras, somewhere near to the fort; such temples were not uncommon in the second and third centuries A.D. The evidence in the case of Lancaster consists of a group of statuary, which was found in 1794 to the south of Lancaster during canal-digging,[22] and evidently not in its original location. One of the heads appears to have the 'Phrygian cap' familiar in Mithraic sculpture. However, an alternative explanation has been put forward that the statues represent a

15. Tile and stone pilae supporting the floor of the bath-house which was located in 1973–4 during the building of Mitre House. (Photograph courtesy of T. W. Potter.)

group from a large mausoleum, which is a possible interpretation of an earth-work at Burrow Heights (about two miles south of the fort), which lies close to the road running south from Lancaster to Walton-le-Dale.[23]

Roman law forbade the burial of the dead *within* settlements, and so, according to custom, burials were placed by the sides of roads leading out of settlements; evidence of cremations has come from the southern end of Penny Street, and of inhumations from West Road. The discovery in Cheapside of a tombstone of a cavalry-

16. The foundation trench for the side wall of a Roman fast-food shop, found under the cellar floor of 65 Church Street in 1973–4. (Photograph courtesy of T. W. Potter.)

soldier, Lucius Julius Apollinaris, may indicate the location nearby of the eastern cemetery, although the stone had itself evidently been re-used for building purposes and may have been moved some distance.

Whilst, therefore, a picture emerges with some detail of an important fort with a thriving civilian settlement, a great deal more work is required to fill in further important detail, and to expand and confirm what are initial impressions. As we shall see later, however, it can be assumed that the presence of a vigorous fort and town at Lancaster will have had implications further afield. Local farmers will have been presented with an opportunity to supply this large market, as well as being in part *required* to supply it through their taxes. Some land will probably have been confiscated and used by the cavalry-unit itself to grow fodder and bedding for its horses, whilst still more will have been appropriated for use as discharge-gratuities for retiring soldiers, such as Julius Januarius;[24] this soldier, who was settled about a mile to the north of the fort, displayed his integration into the society and economy of the lower Lune valley by making a dedication to Jalonus Contrebis, who was, in all probability, the Romano-Celtic spirit of the river Lune, on whose continuing favour soldier and civilian alike depended.

17. Group of Roman statuary which was found, deliberately buried in a pit, during the building of the Lancaster Canal to the south of the town in 1794. (G. Harris.)

Name and garrisons

There is no direct evidence of the Roman name for Lancaster, although it is likely that *Iter* X of the *Antonine Itinerary* preserves a sequence in the Lune valley (see Shotter, 1993, 105–9). If so, the name was probably *Calacum*, which is perhaps also the *Caluvio* of the *Ravenna Cosmography*.

Units of the Roman army associated with Lancaster:

Legion ?	Fragmentary tile-stamp (Shotter and White, 1990, 64f).
Ala Augusta	*RIB* 606 (probably of early second-century date).
Ala Sebosiana	*RIB* 605 (dated to A.D. 262); tile-stamps from Lancaster and Quernmore (Shotter and White, 1990, 63–5); lead sealing (Shotter and White, 1990, 65).
Numerus Barcariorum	*RIB* 601 (third and/or fourth century in date).

18. The tombstone of a former trooper of the Ala Sebosiana found at Worms on the Rhine. The unit may well have been brought to Britain from Germany in about A.D. 69. (Photograph courtesy of B. J. N. Edwards, County Archaeologist for Lancashire.)

Note on Visible Remains

a) *Western Vicarage Field*: clear traces can be seen of earth-works representing a rampart-system. Although these earth-works are known to have been of medieval origin, excavation has shown that they precisely overlie the north-west corner of the defences of the enlarged Roman fort.

b) *Northern Vicarage Field*: the remains of a stone-built bath-house have been consolidated here: they represent the underfloor-level (hypocaust) of a warm or hot room in the bath-house; adjacent to this room – the *tepidarium* – is a smaller room which was probably

the plunge-bathroom of this part of the suite. Both rooms were served by the same furnace-area. The *tepidarium* was destroyed in the Roman period by the building of the new fourth-century fort; the remains of this – the Wery Wall – can be seen a little to the north of the *tepidarium*. These remains constitute the core of a polygonal bastion which stood probably on the northern corner of this fort.

The bath-house was part either of a *mansio* (hotel) or of a courtyard-house, built presumably to house a significant official.

c) *Lancaster City Museum*: the Museum contains a collection of pottery and other finds from Lancaster itself and from neighbouring sites such as Burrow-in-Lonsdale, Quernmore and Warton Crag. The collection includes most of the inscriptions from Lancaster listed in Shotter and White, 1990, 58–63, as well as the Hadrianic milestone from Caton and part of a triangular tombstone from Burrow-in-Lonsdale (Edwards, 1971).

d) *Roman roads*: although a number of the City's streets and alleys probably have a Roman origin, such as those which link Church Street with Market Street, the chief surviving road-lines are represented by Church Street (the continuation of the road out of the east gate), and Penny Street (which was probably the main road to the north, from which a spur led to the fort itself).

19. Professor Ian Richmond surveys a trench in Vicarage Field in 1950.

Notes to Chapter 3

1. For a full treatment of the discovery and interpretation of Roman Lancaster, see Shotter and White, 1990. Excavations since 1950 are discussed in Jones and Shotter, 1988, and also in Geoffrey Leather's privately published *Roman Lancaster: Some Excavation Reports and some Observations* (Preston 1972).
2. For relevant passages, see Shotter and White, 1990, pp. 6 and 33.
3. See Penney, 1981.
4. The locations of these are given in Shotter and White, 1990, 11–12.
5. *Life of Agricola* 20, 2.
6. Jones M. J., 1975.
7. The evidence is discussed in Shotter, 1994.
8. *RIB* 606 (*Ala Augusta*); *RIB* 605 (*Ala Sebosiana*). In general, see Shotter and White, 1990, 27-31.
9. *RIB* 604; dating to c.A.D. 102.
10. *RIB* 605; see Jones and Shotter, 1988, 208–11.
11. For the sealing from western Vicarage Field, see Shotter and White, 1990, 65; for that from Brough-under-Stainmore, see Richmond, 1936, 120. The reference from Carlisle is *Tab. Luguv.* 19 (See I. D. Caruana, *The Roman Forts at Carlisle;*

20. A small hoard of third-century coins found, still wrapped in a piece of cloth, at the rear of St George's Quay in 1992. The weave of the cloth was preserved in the corrosion-products of the bronze coins. (Lancaster City Museums.)

Excavations at Annetwell Street, 1973–84 [forthcoming].) Other references to the unit may be seen in the discharge-diploma found at Malpas in Cheshire (*CIL* XVI. 48), on a tombstone from Worms on the Rhine (*ILS* 2533) and on a dedication from Co. Durham (*RIB* 1041) which records a successful boar-hunting expedition by the unit's commander.

12. Shotter and White, 1990, 64f.
13. *RIB* 602; for the duties of these seconded legionaries, see Birley A., 1979, 86ff.
14. *RIB* 616 and 617: both statuettes are now lost.
15. *RIB* 601; See Shotter, 1973.
16. The sites from which generalisations are often made are Vindolanda (see Birley R, 1977) and Manchester (see Jones, 1974). For the proposition of upgrading see Arrian, *Periplus* 7. 4 – 8. 1.
17. Jones and Shotter, 1988, 61–71.
18. Jones and Shotter, 1988, 160–6.
19. *RIB* 602.
20. *RIB* 605; see Jones and Shotter, 1988, 72–6.
21. Shotter and White, 1990, 32–46.
22. Watkin, 1883, 180f.
23. Edwards, 1971.
24. *RIB* 600.

Chapter 4

Burrow-in-Lonsdale

BURROW lies on rising ground on the edge of the Lune flood-plain and not far from the Leck Beck. There is little to show today of its Roman past and most people pass the site, marked by a dangerous double bend in the road, without a sideways glance. However, earlier antiquaries were aware of its Roman significance and recorded evidence which is now lost. The first of these was John Leland, writing in about 1540. He wrote:

> "Burrow now a vyllage, set in Lunesdale a vi myles beneth the foote of Dentdale, hath beene by likelyhood sum notable town. The plough menne find there yn ering [ploughing] *lapides quadratos* [squared stones] and many other straung thinges; and this place is much spoken of, of the inhabitants there." [1]

Later in the same century William Camden wrote:

> "As soone as *Lune* is entred into Lancashire, *Lacc*, a little brooke from out of the East, joyneth his streame with it. In which place now standeth *Over-Burrow*, a very small village of husbandmen; which, as the inhabitants enformed mee, had been sometimes a great City, and took up all those large fields between *Lacce* and *Lone*, and after it had suffered all miseries that follow famine, was driven to composition through extremity. This tradition they received from their ancestours, delivered as it were from hand to hand unto them. And in very truth by divers and sundry monuments exceeding ancient, by engraven stones, pavements of square checker worke, peeces of Roman coine, and by this new name *Burrow*, which with us signifieth a *Burgh*, that place should seeme to bee of great antiquity." [2]

At the very end of the seventeenth century Rev. Thomas Machell, rector of Kirkby Thore in Westmorland, called here in his search for material for a book on Cumberland and Westmorland. Although he died before it could be completed his notes survive in the Dean and Chapter Library at Carlisle and were published in 1963 under the title of *Antiquary on Horseback*.[3] Machell records several inscriptions which clearly came from the fort or the civilian settlement, as well as one which was in his day at Kirkby Lonsdale but is now lost. The Kirkby Lonsdale inscription, and another in Tunstall church, are almost certainly from the fort at Burrow.

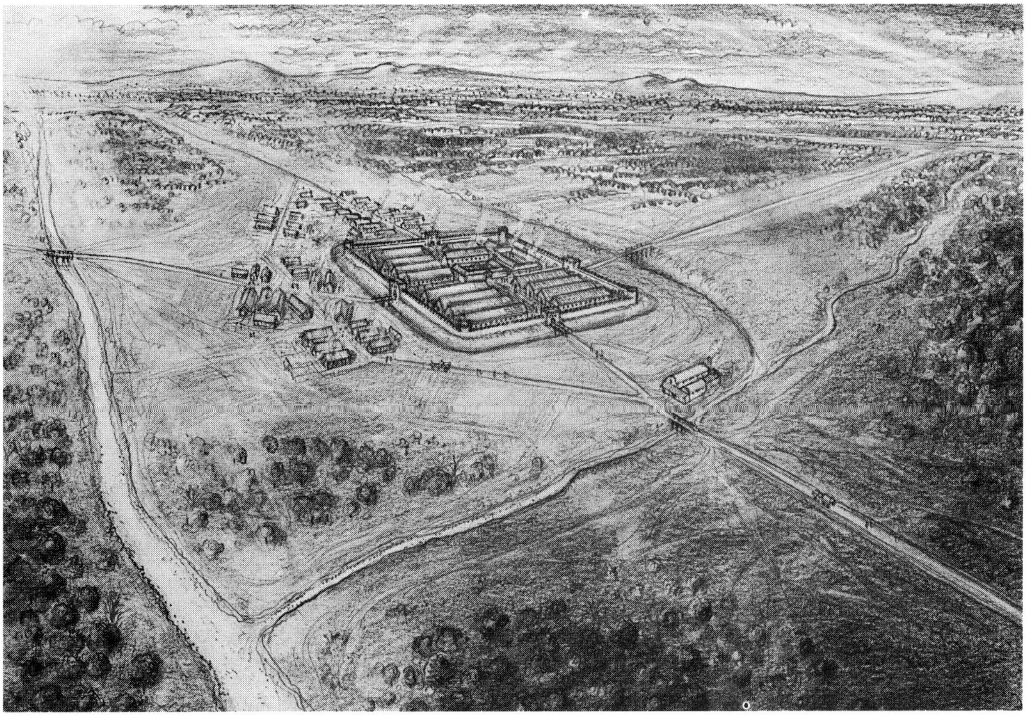

21. Reconstruction drawing by David Vale of the Roman fort of Burrow-in-Lonsdale, as it may have looked from the south-west in the second century A.D. The position of the civilian settlement to the north and west is more or less determined by the lack of flat ground elsewhere. It is likely that the bath-house lay in the valley of the Leck Beck, to the south of the fort. Such is the depth of the ravine to the east that the road may have been carried on a trestle bridge.

It was not until 1746 that anything further was recorded about Burrow. In that year a book entitled *Antiquitates Bremetonacenses or The Roman Antiquities of Overborough*[4] appeared. It was written by another clergyman, Rev. Richard Rauthmel, and likewise appeared posthumously. A second edition appeared in 1824, published by Arthur Foster of Kirkby Lonsdale. The occasion for the book was the rebuilding of Burrow Hall by Rauthmel's patron and university friend Robert Fenwick, whose family had acquired the property in about 1690 from Col. Briggs. This revealed surprisingly little about the fort. As Prof. Eric Birley said in 1946, 'seldom can so large a book have been made out of so little material'. Rev. T. D. Whitaker was of similar opinion in 1823 when he wrote of Rauthmel, 'His experience of Roman antiquities was not equal to his zeal, and his imagination often got the better of his judgement'. A correspondent to the *Gentleman's Magazine* in 1759 [5] had a similar view; 'Mr. Rauthmell . . . is but a bad writer, and, I think, no better an antiquarian'.

Rauthmel's book probably had a very limited currency. Visitors to the area in the eighteenth and early nineteenth century would probably have been aware of the fort through Hutton's *Tour to the Caves in the West-Riding of Yorkshire*, which appeared as an addendum to later editions of Thomas West's popular *Guide to the Lakes*, devoting several pages to Burrow. As well as beautiful prospects, the

22. It was the rebuilding of Burrow Hall, seen here in an engraving by Havell after Stirzaker, which led to the rediscovery of the Roman fort on the site. The house follows very closely the alignment of the fort.
(Lancaster City Museums.)

hall and grounds offered an added frisson to the sensitive visitor by its Roman connections.

> " . . . Our ideas of the beauties of art and nature were mellowed and refined by those of venerable antiquity. We were now on classic ground; *Overborough* being most undoubtedly a Roman station and garrison . . ." [6]

Although Burrow has long been known to be a Roman site, no-one knew where the fort or its civilian settlement actually lay until the excavations of the 1950s. The whereabouts of the civilian settlement can now be surmised, but its extent is still quite unknown. Since the site of the fort occupies a bluff above the Leck Beck to its south and east the area left for level and extensive settlement is reduced to the north and west. Some evidence of Roman activity has come from fruitless searches for the fort itself to the north. Behind the Hall, to the east, is a steep ravine which offered a natural defence to the fort and a romantic prospect to the later house.

To the west are level fields stretching to the river Lune, and it is here that the focus of the civilian settlement is likely to have been. A number of coins and some pottery have been found in this area, including a lion-head mortarium, and further west on the bank of the Lune. One might expect civilian buildings to spread in ribbon-fashion along roads; so a prime candidate for the 'main street' of the *vicus* would be along the line of the road postulated to have run from the fort at Burrow, across the Lune in a north-westerly direction towards Whittington and ultimately to the fort at Watercrook.[7]

Excavations

A number of small-scale excavations have taken place on the site as well as the main excavations of 1952–3, which revealed most of what we know of the layout of the fort. In chronological order these are:

1905 Anthony Moorhouse, a plumber from Kirkby Lonsdale and amateur antiquary, excavated mainly to the north of the fort, perhaps within the civilian settlement, but probably also located its north wall. In addition he may have dug to the west of the site. One of his finds (see below) was a bronze ox-head from a cauldron or bucket. It was believed at one time to have come from a Romano-British site at Sealford but Moorhouse's notes make it clear that it came from Burrow. These manuscript notes were recently given to Lancaster City Museum by Mr. North of Yealand Conyers.

1947 Trial trenches were dug by Lt. Col. O. H. North and E. J. W. Hildyard to the north and north-west of Burrow Hall, and therefore, as we now know, outside the area of the fort. The whereabouts of the finds are unknown.[8]

23. Aerial photograph of Burrow Hall and the hamlet of Over Burrow from the west. The prominent drive to the Hall represents the line of the main east–west road inside the fort, which occupies the wooded area to the left and part of the meadow to the centre of the photograph. (Photograph courtesy of A. C. H. Olivier, Lancaster University Archaeological Unit.)

1952–3 Fuller excavations by the same excavators over two seasons totalling about five weeks revealed enough detail to enable the location of all the fort-walls and of the north and south gates to be plotted. Work started in 1952 most opportunely with the location of the south gate in the gardens to the south-west of the Hall. Once this had been located the standardisation of the plan of Roman forts came to the rescue, enabling the excavators correctly to predict the whereabouts of the walls, not only the south wall of the fort but also the east and west walls.[9]

In 1953 attention was turned to the northern defences. Here the wall was found more or less as predicted, but unexpectedly a ditch on a different alignment, belonging probably to an earlier fort or to an annexe, also came to light. The north gate, like the south gate a double one with guard towers in the standard positions, was also located.

The fort thus defined is almost square in plan, which, although similar to Lancaster, is unusual and not rendered essential by the topography. The east and west walls are located by very small amounts of evidence from very small trenches. It is possible that internal walls were misconstrued as fort walls, which would allow the fort to be a rectangle with its longer axis east-west, or that buildings outside the fort were located in one or more of these trenches, and that the fort was a rectangle with its longer axis north-south. Only further area-excavation would answer these points. It must be remembered that the excavation-work was carried out using very narrow trenches at key points only, in the manner of its time; so evidence for earlier, larger or smaller forts may have been overlooked, and nothing at all was found of the internal layout of the fort. The area defined by these walls totals almost five acres, somewhat larger than usual and capable of accommodating five hundred cavalry and their mounts, or one thousand infantry, or mixed elements of two or more units.

The earliest pottery found on the site was of Flavian date but most of the structural evidence was thought by the excavators to belong to the third or early fourth centuries A.D.. However, anomalous ditches and timber posts suggested that earlier, timber, forts had lain on a slightly different alignment and occupied a different area. The interior of the fort was not examined so no internal buildings were located. The layout and dating of these must therefore be quite conjectural and it would be unsound to date the whole fort upon the phasing of its defences.

One discovery which, in retrospect, is of greater interest to us than it was to the excavators is that of a small square building, oddly aligned to the ramparts and occupying part of the roadway of the south gate. Late blockings of double gateways are not at all unusual, particularly upon Hadrian's Wall, but the way in which this building is set askew to the gateway is reminiscent of recent discoveries at

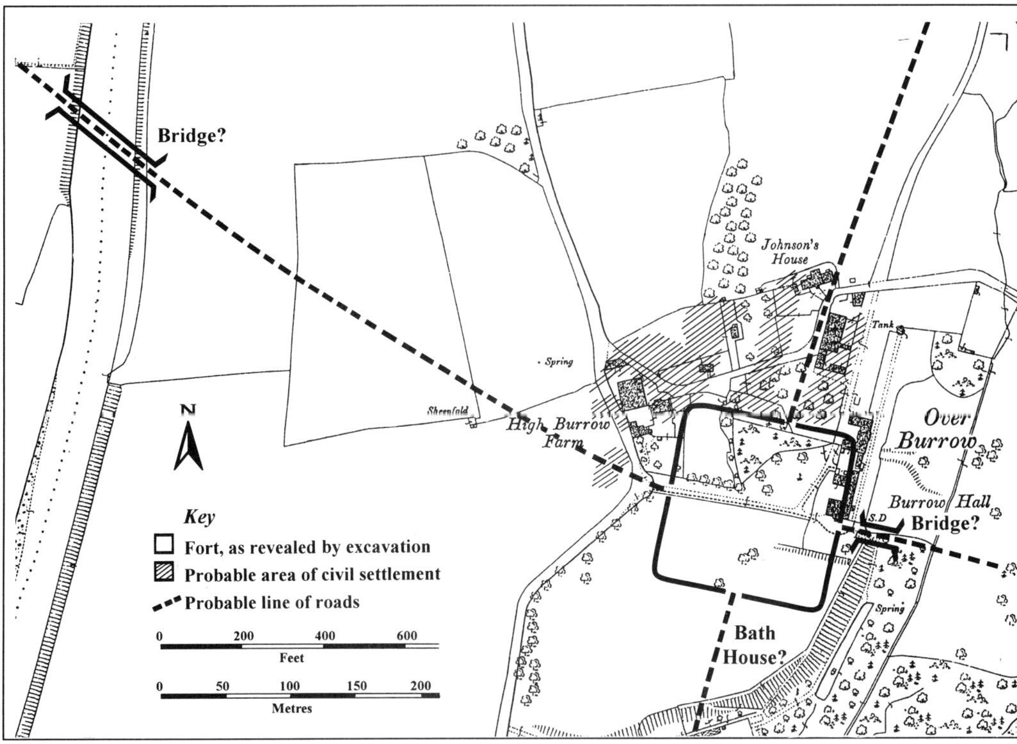

24. Plan of the fort at Burrow-in-Lonsdale based on the 25-inch Ordnance Survey map, excavation plans by the late E. J. W. Hildyard and more recent research. (P. Thompson/W. Moore after Hildyard & Pinfold; reproduced by courtesy of the Council of the Cumberland & Westmorland Antiquarian & Archaeological Society.)

Birdoswald where a very long and significant sub-Roman occupation, including reuse of a gateway, has been recognised. Many earlier excavations may have missed altogether this kind of evidence or else ignored it as being 'late' and therefore of no interest. Dating material for this is totally lacking, unfortunately. However, should further excavation take place at Burrow in the future evidence of late- and sub-Roman activity will be a high research priority.

1974 Dr. T. W. Potter carried out very limited machine-trenching in advance of building work to the north-east of the fort. Nothing of significance was revealed, either of the fort or civilian settlement. There are no recorded finds.[10]

It is of interest to examine the relationship between the Hall, its main drive and the alignment of the fort. It can hardly be a coincidence that the hall seems to lie along the eastern defences or that the drive seems to reflect the main east-west Roman road. In all probability the Hall's location and alignment were determined by the earlier house on the site, and that this in turn was influenced by Roman walls and ditches – and possibly even by the east gate – when the remains stood much higher.

25. Colonel and Mrs North at the south gate of Burrow fort in 1952.

Colonel North in a trench on the northern defences of Burrow fort, 1953. The stables of the Hall are in the background.

Significant Finds

Gold bulla A small gold *bulla* or pendant was found, according to Rauthmel, 'in the fortress [of Burrow] by Miss Fenwick'. He does not record the circumstances. Because of its unusual nature it is particularly regrettable that it no longer seems to exist. The drawing which Rauthmel adds to his account does not give much help. The object appears to be of spherical shape, with a fixing at the top to allow it to be strung round the neck. Yates, writing in 1851,

26.

27.

26. Part of the north wall of the fort during excavation, 1952–3. (Above right) An oak post found embedded under the roadway of the north gate at Burrow.

27. Details of the south gateway at Burrow, 1953, showing the misaligned and probably late building occupying the site of the western guardroom. (P. Thompson/W. Moore after Hildyard.)

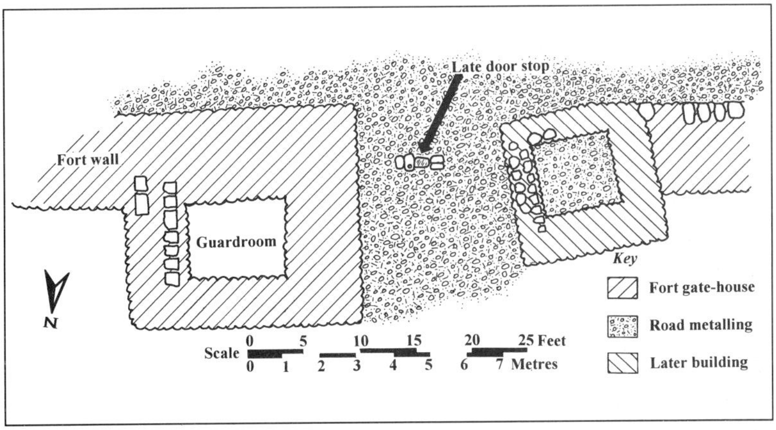

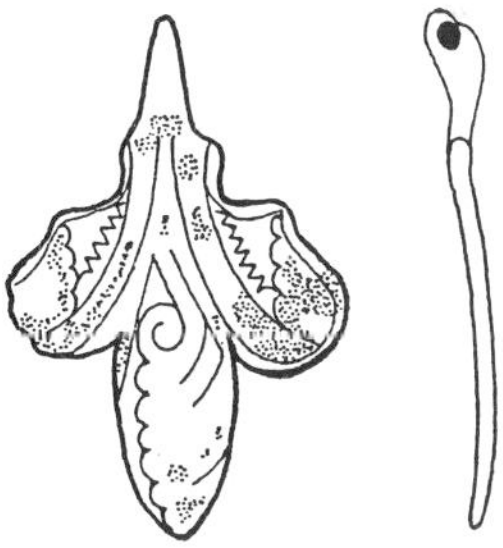

28.

28. Bronze horse-trapping found at Overtown in 1984. (Drawing courtesy of B. J. N. Edwards, County Archaeologist for Lancashire.)

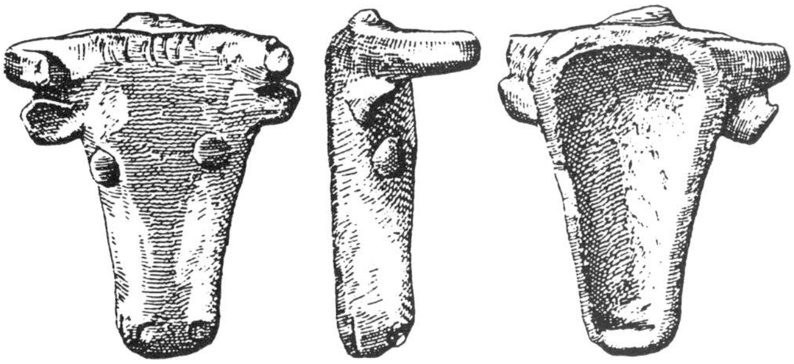

29.

29. Bronze ox-head escutcheon found at Burrow in 1905. (By permission of the Society of Antiquaries.)

30. Two sides of the carved capital found in the grounds of Burrow Hall before 1824. One side is carved with foliage, the other three with human or cherubic faces.

suggested that such *bullae* were specifically worn by Roman boys – (presumably those of high status) – and the other examples he gives indicate that the normal form was that of a flat disc with a tubular top for stringing.[11]

Horse-trapping The discovery of a horse-trapping in the shape of a gilt copper-alloy trilobed pendant at Overtown in 1984, kindly brought to our attention by B. J. N. Edwards, probably signifies the presence of horses at the nearby fort. This does not have to indicate that the garrison was of cavalry, since any garrison would include mounts for officers and couriers, as well as 'unofficial' horses.

Bronze Ox head The *Antiquaries Journal* for 1935 illustrates a bronze ox-head, which was thought at that time to have come from the native settlement at Sealford, near Kirkby Lonsdale. It is apparent from Anthony Moorhouse's notes that it was in fact discovered at Burrow in 1905. Most probably it came from the civilian area to the north of the fort. Although it is a relatively crude example of the type it is one of a series not uncommon in the north and may have been attached to a large bucket or cauldron, along with representations of other animal and perhaps human heads.[12]

Carved capital Although there is no published illustration of the carved capital before 1930 [13] it is clear from Anthony Moorhouse's manuscript notes (*c.*1909) that it had been unearthed some years previous to that date. In fact the 1824 edition of Rauthmel [14] seems to refer to the find '. . . said to have been dug up at the time the garden ground was trenched.' The exact circumstances of its discovery are unknown. Birley [15] concludes that it must come from a temple or shrine and not from within the fort area, but it might, of course, have been taken from derelict civilian buildings and incorporated into the fort at a late date. It has carved human or divine faces on three of its sides, astonishingly similar to the cherubs which decorate many seventeenth-century gravestones. It is of exceptional interest but seems until now to have escaped the text-books.

Marble In the excavation of 1952 a small piece of green marble was found in the make-up of the roadway of the south gate. It has been identified as 'Campan Vert' from the Pyrenees. From its position it may originally have formed part of an inscription set above the gate, rather than being an object in its own right such as a slab of the type used by Roman eye-doctors. Nonetheless it serves to underline the widespread and exotic sources of building materials in even such a frontier fort as this. No marble has yet been found in the much more extensive excavations at Lancaster.

Coins Only a handful of Roman coins are recorded as having been found at the fort and civilian settlement of Burrow, and the sample is not sufficiently large or well-provenanced to be of much use. Of the twenty-seven recorded, thirteen are of the Antonine period and the earliest and latest are of Vespasian and Constantius I respectively. Most interestingly, no coins at all of the third century have yet been recorded there – statistically one would have expected these to be the commonest type – so this may signify an unusual pattern of occupation of the site.[16]

The Name and Garrisons

Although Rauthmell believed this fort was *Bremetonnacum* modern scholars unite in applying this to Ribchester. Instead, *Calacum* has been suggested.[17] If, however, Lancaster is to be identified with *Calacum* then Burrow could be *Alauna*.[18]

The inscriptions give no help in identifying the garrison but the size of the fort at nearly five acres could accommodate five hundred cavalry, one thousand infantry, or some less conventional mixed brigading.

Visible Remains

A fragment of *RIB* 612 can still be seen built into a barn on the east side of the road, just to the north of the entrance to Burrow Hall. It stands out because of its reddish colour against the grey of the other stones.

Although the fort has influenced the layout of the Hall and its park there is nothing to be seen at ground level. The Hall and its grounds are private property; there is no right of access.

Location of Finds

Lancaster City Museum contains some of the finds from the 1952–3 excavations as well as part of the gabled tombstone *RIB* 612. Kendal Museum has two restored flagons from the 1952–3 excavations.

Notes to Chapter 4

1. Toulmin-Smith, 1910, 5, 46
2. Camden, 1610
3. Ewbank, 1963
4. Rauthmel, 1749
5. Gemsege, 1759, 407–8
6. West, 1784, 240
7. Villy, 1937, 49
8. North, Hildyard and Gillam, 1948, 23–41
9. Hildyard, 1954, 66–101
10. Potter, 1975, 376
11. Yates, 1851, 166–71
12. *Ant. J.*, xxxiv, 1954, 225; Toynbee, 1964, 124; MacGregor, 1976, 155 and Fig. 313
13. Collingwood, 1930, 216–7
14. Rauthmel, 1824, 137
15. Birley, 1946, 142n
16. Shotter, 1990, 13–4
17. Rivet and Smith, 1979, 170–2, 288
18. Shotter, 1993, 107–9

Chapter 5

Low Borrow Bridge

THE fort, usually known as Castlehows or Low Borrow Bridge, which stands at the head of the Lune gorge at Tebay, presents us with something of a paradox. Visually, few Roman forts have better retained the integrity of their physical outlines: yet, our knowledge of the history and development of the site is notably inadequate.[1] Little excavation has taken place, and, in contrast with most other Roman sites in the north-west, few finds have been recorded. The rural setting of Low Borrow Bridge has both to an extent protected it and at the same time served to preserve its mystery.

The early antiquarians,[2] such as Camden, Leland and Horsley, appear not to have noticed the site at all; further, even its earliest notice – in the late eighteenth century – failed to recognise the site

31. It was the Lancaster & Carlisle Railway which initially opened up the Lune gorge. The rural fastnesses of Low Borrow Bridge are shown here by the *Illustrated London News* for 26 December 1846, when the line was opened.

32. (Left and opposite) Three illustrations showing the western gate, east wall and eastern gate of Low Borrow Bridge fort as excavated in 1883. (Reproduced by courtesy of the Council of the Cumberland & Westmorland Antiquarian & Archaeological Society.)

as of Roman origin. It was not until the early nineteenth century that this identification was made.[3] Nonetheless, it would appear from the name, Borrow Beck, that there had been a long-term recollection of the presence of a fortified site. A number of accounts appeared during the nineteenth century, which established some features of the site, and recorded a small number of finds.

Features which were noted included the presence of two ditches on the fort's western side, a hypocaust inside the northern part of the fort, and a bridge-abutment and a stretch of road to the north at the crossing of Borrow Beck. It was assumed that the site was *Alone* of *Iter* X of the *Antonine Itinerary*, and the objective of the first excavations, in 1883, was to recover inscribed stones which might throw conclusive light on the name of the site.[4] This period of work

did not produce inscriptions, but did indicate some curious features of the site; for example, a survey indicated that the fort was in fact a parallelogram rather than a true rectangle, and observation suggested that there was no gateway in the southern rampart. The eastern gateway was recognised as a normal construction of two carriage-ways, and its western equivalent was assumed – probably wrongly – to be of similar type. Such lack of symmetry between the side-gateways can be paralleled, for example, at Vindolanda. Similarly, Birley has cited Bainbridge as a parallel for the absence of a gateway in one wall – at least until very late in the occupation.[5] This work also identified a building off the fort's south-east corner, which is probably the bath-house.[6] Further work, though unfortunately never published, was carried out in the 1930s on the area of the north gate and on the south-east angle. In the former area, it was shown that the north wall had undergone a late rebuilding which had obliterated

33. Aerial photographs from the south-east showing (above) a general view of Low Borrow Bridge fort and (left) a close-up which brings out the western ditches. (Photographs by courtesy of G. D. B. Jones/Manunair.)

the gateway, whilst the latter part of the site indicated a complex chronology.[7]

The fort itself is well sited, although some have thought that a stronger position could have been found a little further north, and closer to Tebay, as is the case with the nearby Norman motte-and-bailey castle. It is protected on the northern and eastern sides by the confluence of the Borrow Beck with the river Lune. To the west of the fort, the fells rise sharply to 1500 feet, and those on the eastern side of the valley achieve a similar height. Roads run northwards to Brougham and south to Burrow-in-Lonsdale, whilst to the west the fort is connected by road with both Watercrook and Ambleside. The size of the visible fort is a little less than three acres which would offer sufficient accommodation for a *cohors quingenaria equitata* (a five-hundred-strong infantry unit with a cavalry-element); the presence of this type of unit is apparently confirmed by one of the two surviving tombstones from the cemetery, which lies a little under a mile to the south. One stone, which was broken up in order to construct a bridge across an unidentified beck, is said to have have depicted a mounted soldier spearing a fallen enemy, and to have contained 'XX' in its inscription – presumably part of the soldier's length of service or age at death.

There is no record of the existence of a civilian settlement other than the probable bath-house at the south-east corner, although the flat meadowland to the south of the fort has been regarded as a suitable situation for one. Further, the confirmation of the existence of a cemetery [8] about a mile south of the fort lends weight to the suggestion that the civilian settlement lay between it and the fort's southern rampart. Various suggestions have placed the parade-ground on meadowland either to the south or the north of the fort, though there is no certainty with regard to this.

Problems concerning the chronology and anatomy of the fort remain, though some progress was made as a result of further excavation in 1950.[9] There seems to be little doubt that activity continued at the site into the late fourth century and beyond; indeed, it was long ago noticed that the remoteness of the spot may well have encouraged the survival of a 'sub-Roman' (or semi-Romanised) community in what remained of the site. Features such as the removal of the north gate and the blocking of the north carriageway of the east gate[10] represent attempts to enhance the protection of the fort-area, which are readily paralleled at other sites. Indeed, some such activity may also explain the apparent absence of a south gate. Late fourth-century pottery was well-represented in the excavations of 1950, especially at the south-east corner.[11] Although no sign was found there of an angle-tower, disturbances in the area which were dated to the late Roman period were considered consistent with the insertion of a platform, now vanished, to accommodate a piece of artillery.

Thus, although detail is sparing, we can regard occupation in the

43. Low Borrow Bridge fort from the south as it may have looked in the second century A.D.; reconstruction drawing by David Vale.

second half of the fourth century as certain, and connected with significant alterations to the fabric of the fort. Excavations have detected at least three phases of activity earlier than this, and have shown with little doubt that the *visible* remains do not represent the fort's earliest phase. The presence of a ditch-like feature *inside* the western rampart, and of post-holes apparently running beneath the fort-wall at the south-east corner suggest strongly that a presumably smaller fort, perhaps broadly sharing a part of the southern and eastern ramparts with its successor, pre-dated the visible structure. Pottery from this early level, though not *closely* datable, clearly derives from the Flavian period. It would appear natural, as the Lune-corridor represents the obvious route from Chester to Carlisle, to assign the earliest fort at Low Borrow Bridge to a date at least as early as Agricola's governorship, if not to that of Cerialis. The survival of posts within the post-holes suggests that, with modern dating-methods, the question of dating the earliest fort should in time be capable of resolution.

Having seen so little of the early fort it is difficult to determine how many phases it had; however, the layout of post-holes[12] is suggestive of more than a single phase. In this case, it may be appropriate to refer the reconstruction and enlarging of the fort to the Trajanic or Hadrianic periods. It can be seen from the spacing of the gateways along the eastern and western ramparts that the fort faced

35. Dressed sandstone blocks facing the wall of the bath-house outside Low Borrow Bridge fort. (Photograph courtesy of J. Anstee.)

towards the south – unless, of course, it had six gates and two more remain to be located in the eastern and western ramparts. If the fort indeed was orientated towards the south, then the absence of a south gate would appear perverse. If there indeed was no south gate, then the impressive eastern gate, which had the closest access to the main north-south route, may have been used as the fort's principal entrance.

The visible fort has signs of two ditches on its southern, western and northern flanks, although some reports have claimed to have identified as many as four on the western side. It is, of course, perfectly possible, as at the fort at Watercrook,[13] that ditches might have been combined with other obstacles, such as palisades and stone-banks. No obvious trace of extended defences remains on the eastern side of the fort. The excavations of 1950 recognised on the western side two phases of clay-rampart fronted by a stone-wall, which appeared to be of a single build with the earliest rampart, rather than, as sometimes happens, pre-dating it.

The pottery suggested that the first clay-rampart should be placed relatively early in the second century and certainly not later than the Hadrianic period. The only indication of date for the second phase of clay-rampart was a little-worn *denarius* of Commodus (A.D. 180–92), which underlay the second phase. This might suggest a Severan date for the refurbishment, although it has been suggested that the structural quality of the east gate points towards significant reconstruction in the late third century under the orders of Constantius I. On present evidence it is impossible to produce a more precise chronology, nor to tell whether (or when) the fort may have temporarily lost its garrison as troop-dispositions were reviewed. However, the cemetery excavations of 1991 demonstrated that, at some point in the third century, the site suffered from major flooding.

36. Excavations in 1991 revealed the Roman cemetery at Low Borrow Bridge. The burial plots (above) can be identified by the darker soil of their ditches.

(Left) A burial urn containing a cremation.
(Photograph courtesy of Lancaster University Archaeological Unit.)

The fort-wall, which has been heavily robbed, was evidently faced with good-quality ashlar; some of the surviving stones displayed diamond-broaching perhaps to prevent rain-water – a constant problem at this site – from standing in the joints; similar stonework treated in this way was observed in 1975 in the bath-house. Such

37. Tombstone of Aelia Sentica erected by her husband Aurelius Verulus, from the Roman cemetery at Low Borrow Bridge. (Drawing by P. Lee by courtesy of Lancaster University Archaeological Unit.)

stone would have needed to be imported from some distance, the nearest source being Orton Low Moor, or Shap. Local slates and river boulders were used for the wall-core, which was bound together with a runny mortar, and for foundations.

Little is known of internal buildings, although one with a hypocaust, reported in the northern portion of the fort, might represent either the commander's house (*praetorium*) or a feature inserted into the headquarters (*principia*). The general absence, however, of reported internal buildings may reflect the fact that, because good-quality ashlar was hard to acquire, many of the internal buildings may have been built of timber or at least have been half-timbered.

As we have noted, it has been generally assumed that the civilian settlement was situated to the south, and perhaps to the east, of the fort, possibly taking as an asset close proximity to the main road. The boggy state of the ground to the west would appear to preclude settlement in that area. The only extra-mural building about which there is any information is the bath-house, which is situated off the fort's south-east corner. It appeared to have been faced with sandstone-blocks, which the excavator attributed to a desire to provide the building with a good appearance.[14] Elements of walls and floors, made of concrete with pounded brick, have been identified, together with a furnace-area. Finds included fragments of box-tiles which carried the heated gases into the walls of the warm and hot rooms. Although a complete plan of the building has not, of course, been recovered, it has been estimated that it was a structure of impressive appearance, possibly with porched entrance-ways, and in the region of fifty-five feet long on its north-south axis. It appears also that the water required both for the bath-house and for the fort itself was channelled on to the site from Birk Knott, on the western side of the valley. The man-made aqueduct has been observed for nearly 600 yards, falling 250 feet in a constant gradient.[15]

A cemetery lay at a distance of almost a mile from the fort; its general siting was already indicated by the discovery of the cavalryman's tombstone, which was mentioned earlier. However,

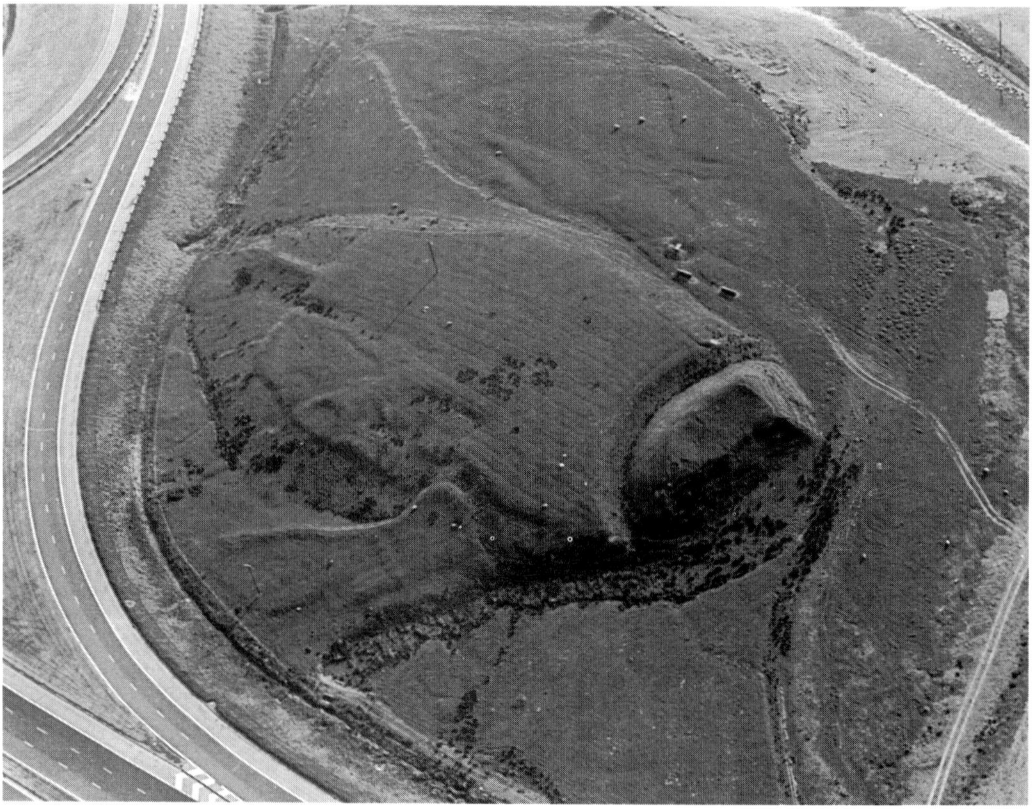

38. The strategic importance of the Lune gorge is underlined by the presence of a Norman motte-and-bailey castle at Tebay, a little north of the Roman fort. Half of the motte has been eroded away by the river Lune. (Photograph courtesy of G. D. B. Jones/Manunair.)

excavation in 1991 [16] recovered a substantial section of the cemetery, revealing sixty-five cremation-pits and twenty cremation-vessels intact. One of these contained a coin, presumably the fee which the deceased person would have had to pay to be ferried across the river Styx. The pits were situated in plots, which were from ten to fifteen feet in diameter and may have been allotted to families or military burial-clubs. Some of these plots cut into others, indicating an extended period of use. One inscription was recovered, a well-cut stone erected by one, Aurelius Verulus, in memory of his wife, Aelia Sentica; the form of her name suggests a British origin, though there was no indication of the couple's occupation.[17]

The cemetery, which was in use apparently between the late-second and mid-fourth centuries, also contained a number of inhumations, apparently in the 'crouch'-position, which was commonly used in Iron-Age Britain.[18]

It is clear that a great deal of work remains to be done to elucidate the chronology, history and development of the fort, together with the nature of its civilian settlement. However, as will be shown in chapter 6, modern research has made considerable progress in providing information about the rural economy which will have been encouraged and enhanced by the existence of this and other forts.

Name of the Site

It was originally assumed that Low Borrow Bridge was the *Alone* of *Iter X* of the *Antonine Itinerary* which is equated with *Alione* of the Notitia Dignitatum and *Alauna* of the Ravenna Cosmography. Although this identification was on the right lines in ascribing *Alone* to the Lune valley, it is in fact more likely that *Galava* of *Iter* X is, in fact, to be identified with Low Borrow Bridge (see Shotter, 1993, 105–9).

Garrisons at the Fort

Cohors quingenaria equitata – at an undetermined date (*RIB* 756)

Note on the Visible Remains

The outline of the larger fort remains visually intact, although most of the stone-work which survives is Roman wall-core or more recent reconstruction. A pair of ditches can be made out on the western side.

The aqueduct-channel can be seen running down the fell-side from NGR SD 604006.

Such finds as have been preserved are stored in Kendal Museum; in recent times excavations were carried out on the fort-site itself in 1950, on the bath-house in 1973, and on the cemetery in 1991.

Notes to Chapter 5

1. The position is best summarised in Birley, 1947; for a convenient summary, see Jones M. J., 1975, 164.
2. Birley, 1947, 1ff.
3. In the *Westmorland Advertiser and Kendal Chronicle* of December 19th, 1812.
4. These are reported in Ferguson, 1886.
5. Birley, 1947, 11–12.
6. Anstee, 1975a.
7. Birley, 1947, 9.
8. For a summary of the cemetery-excavation of 1991, see *Britannia* XXIII (1992), 272: full publication will appear in Lambert *et al.*, 1995.
9. Hildyard and Gillam, 1951.
10. See *RCHM, (Westmorland),* 100.
11. Hildyard and Gillam, 1951, 49.
12. See the plan in Hildyard and Gillam, 1951, 48.
13. See the plan in Potter, 1979, 151.
14. Anstee, 1975a.
15. Anstee, 1975b.
16. For a summary, see *Britannia* XXIII (1992), 272.
17. See *Britannia* XXIII (1992), 312f.
18. Lambert *et al.*, 1995.

Chapter 6

Roads, Industry and Farmers

THE Roman forts in the Lune valley were intended to act as centres for 'police-forces'; such a function must at first have been vital for security reasons, but in the long term will have continued to be necessary to ensure the stable development of a Romanised economy. Essential to these troops, of course, was an efficient system of communications. However, just as essential was a developing industrial and agricultural landscape to service the requirements of the troops. Whilst some manufacturing could be provided in larger centres such as Wilderspool (near Warrington) and distributed through army-depots, such as Walton-le-Dale (near Preston), much remained locally-based – in the civilian settlements and in the broader hinterland (*territorium*) of each fort. Viewed from the other side, the presence of these well-paid troops was a stimulus to local people – manufacturers and farmers – to produce not just what was needed to provide for themselves and to pay their taxes, but also a realistic surplus that could be taken to the centres of population, and sold for profit, or bartered. Over the period, therefore, during which Roman troops occupied the Lune valley, we may assume that there was steady social and economic development, aided by the retirement and settling of Romanised troops.

Communications

The river Lune itself will have formed part of the communications-system, and we have already noted the likelihood of a flourishing port at Lancaster, perhaps serviced by the soldiers/lightermen of the *Numerus Barcariorum*. How far inland the river was navigable is hard to say, although the fact that the inscription recording the dedication to Mars by the *Numerus Barcariorum* was actually found at Halton [1] may indicate transportation beyond the tidal reaches (see above, chapter 1). Further, there seems no reason why smaller boats should not have made use of the river further north.

Two major roads ran northwards to the Lune valley – the Lancashire coastal road from Wilderspool and Walton-le-Dale to Lancaster, and the main military road from Chester and Ribchester, which itself became the Lune valley road beyond the fort at Burrow-in-Lonsdale. It is evident that two roads ran in an easterly direction from Lancaster, one on either bank of the Lune.[2]

39. Milestone set up in the reign of the emperor Hadrian, from the Artle Beck at Caton. Now in Lancaster City Museum. (Photograph by G. Harris.)

It appears that the Lancashire coastal road is represented in Lancaster itself by Penny Street, and that the fort on Castle Hill was served by a spur running from it. Initially, at least, the most important of the exit-roads from the fort was that which left the eastern gate and is represented now by Church Street. This road, probably near Stonewell, formed a crossing with the road from the south; from this crossing one road ran in a south-easterly direction, passing the kiln-site at Low Pleasant (Quernmore), whilst the other ran across Lancaster Ridge towards Caton and Brookhouse, passing close to another kiln-site at Lythe Brow. Metalling belonging to this road was observed in 1992 during the laying of a British Gas pipeline near to Gresgarth Hall. The road was running in a north-easterly direction; both to the north-east and south-west of the spot where it was observed, an *agger* can be picked out intermittently on the ground. The road will have crossed Artle Beck, and headed for Brookhouse, and it will be recalled that the fine Hadrianic milestone (now in Lancaster City Museum)[3] was found in Artle Beck in 1803. The stone records a distance of four miles, presumably from Lancaster, though a name cannot be made out on the inscription.

Beyond Brookhouse, another sighting was made in 1992 approximately on the course of the minor road to Hornby. Beyond this, the course is less clear; we may assume that the river was followed to Burrow-in-Lonsdale, and that at some point a branch continued the original north-easterly direction, and making for Bainbridge. This may have occurred immediately north of the river Greta to avoid duplicating river-crossings. If this was the case then we should expect a junction with the main north-south route a little to the east of Cantsfield.

The main thrust of the Lune valley road is from here the north-south route itself, leading through Casterton and Barbon, its course marked by considerable stretches of tracks and modern roads. Near Cowan Bridge, there is by the side of the Roman road a short stump of a cylindrical stone, which now does duty as a parish-boundary marker, but looks very like the remains of a Roman milestone.[4] At Middleton, another, this time well-preserved, milestone can be seen, through re-erected in 1836 some two hundred yards to the east of its original position. The line of the road itself at this point appeared as a linear crop-mark during the drought of 1992; it ran much closer to the river than the present position of the milestone would suggest. The significance of the milestone has been frequently discussed:[5] marking a distance of fifty-three miles, presumably from Carlisle, it has been proposed as a possible indicator of the southern boundary of the *Civitas Carvetiorum*.

From Middleton,[6] the road runs a little to the east of Sedbergh, and then is marked by a modern minor road (known as Howgill Lane) on the steep fellside, closely following the river and heading for the fort at Low Borrow Bridge, and crossing the river a short distance to the south of the fort. It is worth noting in passing a small, square, earthwork with rounded corners on Holme Fell and a circular one near Middleton Hall;[7] these *could* be elements in a system of signalling, or watchtowers, related to the road up the Lune valley.

Beyond the fort, the line of the road has been the subject of much discussion;[8] it would appear to continue on the western side of the river, diverging from it to the north-west of Tebay and making for the clear stretch of road running over Orton Low Moor. The road was in fact sectioned in Sproatgill in 1991,[9] and its foundations shown to have a central spine of heavy boulders, presumably to lend stability in such an exposed environment. The road from here runs towards the fort at Brougham and a junction with the road from York which crosses Stainmore.

40. Roman milestone re-erected at Middleton, a little distance from where it was found, in 1836.

The Lancashire coastal road, which crossed the Lune by a bridge beneath the shadow of Castle Hill, headed north through Bolton-le-Sands for the late Flavian fort at Watercrook. It is almost certain that immediately north of the river, a road branched off in a north-easterly direction to run along the north bank of the Lune. It appears that this ran through Halton and Arkholme towards a fording-place just south of Whittington, thus gaining access to the fort at Burrow-in-Lonsdale.

We may be certain that a substantial collection of minor track-ways led into these principal roads, and thus drew manufacturers and

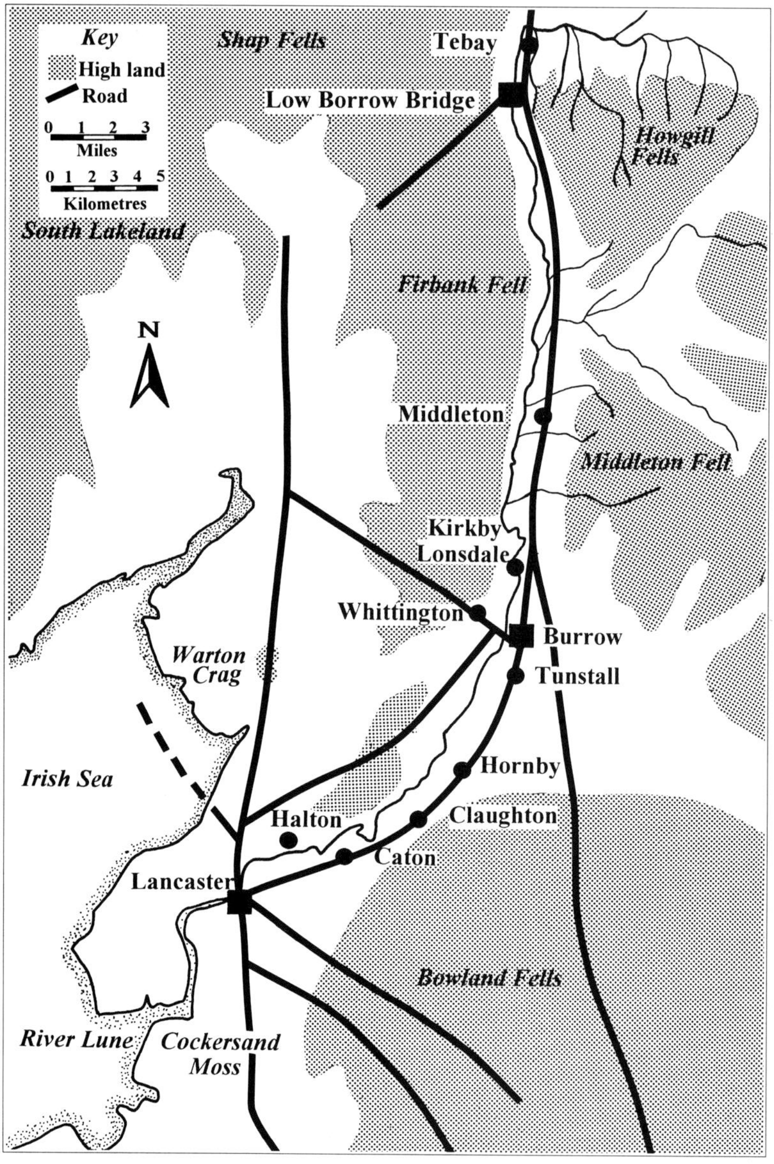

41. Map of Roman roads in the Lune valley. (P. Thompson/W. Moore.)

farmers more closely into the Romanised network. Such trackways may well continue to serve villages and farms, or to be used for moving farm-stock between pastures. Their Roman origin, however, although often strongly suspected, is scarcely capable of proof.

Excavations of Roman Roads

It is notoriously easy to propose a network of Roman roads on little more evidence than a few straight lines on a map and a few chance alignments on the ground. Apart from the few roads which are clearly Roman and the origins of which are not in doubt there are two classes of evidence which can give us a degree of confidence in our attributions.

One of these is the existence of a Roman milestone beside a road or the finding of one in the past, such as at Caton, where a milestone was washed out of the Artle Beck in 1803 at a point where we would predict a road to run, or at Middleton, where a milestone was re-erected near its findspot beside the manifest earthworks of a road.

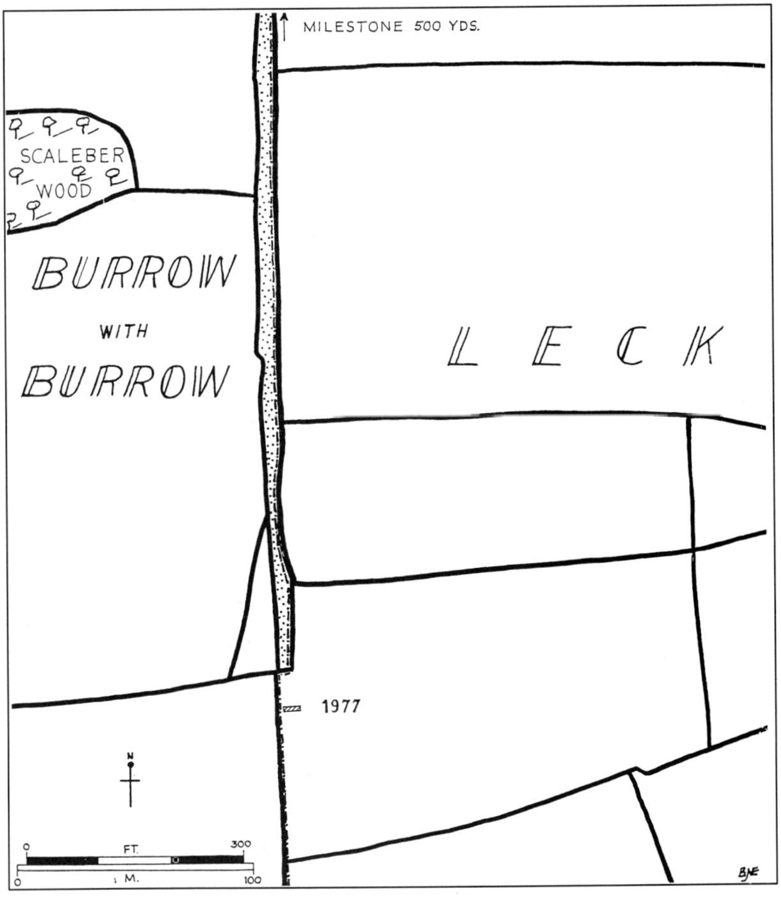

42. Site of the road-section in Leck parish, 1977. (By courtesy of B. J. N. Edwards, County Archaeologist for Lancashire.)

The other is where archaeological cross-sections have been cut through a suspected road-line. The evidence can even then sometimes be ambiguous, especially if the road-material has been quarried away.

Three road-sections have been cut within the Lune valley; at Leck, at Casterton and just short of the fort at Low Borrow Bridge, all on the road numbered 7c by Margary.[10]

Leck, 1977 In May 1977, B. J. N. Edwards cut a section across the line of the Roman road from Manchester to Carlisle at a point some 800 yards south of Overtown. He has very kindly allowed us to use some unpublished illustrations.[11]

South of Overtown the road is a classic example of the stages of abandonment of a former through-route. It ranges from a metalled road to a stony trackway, then to a green lane and finally to a hedgerow still forming the parish boundary between Leck on the east and Burrow-with-Burrow on the west. The section was cut where the green lane has just died out into a hedgerow (SD 63057530).

The Roman road metalling was found to lie partly beneath the hedgerow and so could only be half-sectioned. Soil creep from the higher (Burrow) side had partially obscured the *agger*. The metalling consisted of a layer of cobbles overlying several layers of clay,

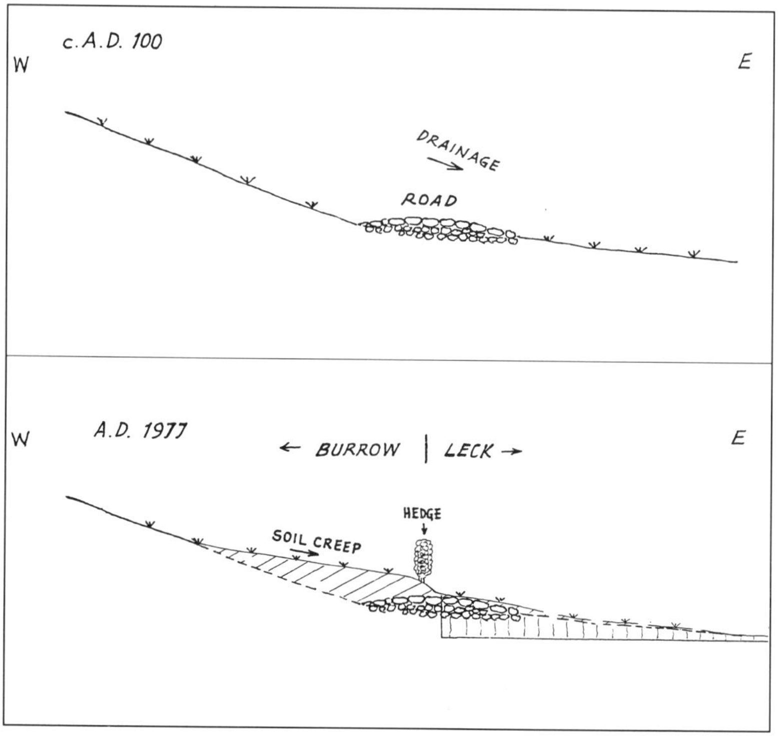

43. Evidence and interpretation: the road-section in Leck parish, 1977. (By courtesy of B. J. N. Edwards, County Archaeologist for Lancashire.)

interleaved with black material, perhaps organic. The cobbles may represent the last resurfacing, since post-medieval pottery was found among them. Alternatively the pottery may be a relic of stone-robbing when the road went out of use here.

Casterton, 1958 The same road was sectioned further north at Casterton (SD626805), by Jane Ewbank in 1958.[12] It was found that the road had been built on a foundation of brushwood to prevent it sinking into the soft subsoil. At the time of excavation the water-table remained high, resulting in excellent preservation of the wood and also of some insect remains. Above this was a layer of river cobbles 22 feet 9 inches across with a surface of tightly packed smaller stones. No paving stones or kerbstones were found, nor was there any evidence for a ditch on either side, but the surface was cambered. It is likely that local ground-conditions affected the construction and details of the road.

Low Borrow Bridge, 1962 This same road was sectioned further north again in 1962 by E. M. L. Macadam at a point just south of Carlingill Beck (SD625994).[13] Here the road known as 'Fairmile', set high on the east side of the Lune Gorge, diverts briefly from the Roman line, allowing a section to be cut without affecting modern traffic. The original line was spotted as a parchmark in dry weather.

Because of the slope of the fellside the foundations needed to be substantial, especially on the downhill side. Large boulders were used, perhaps derived from the nearby beck. The surface had mostly been washed away by water running down the hillside but still consisted of closely packed smaller stones, larger than gravel. The overall width was some 18 feet, narrower than at Casterton.

Industry

As we have already noted, a considerable amount of industry will have been located in the civilian settlements.[14] Many of the 'strip-houses' will have provided both home and business-premises for potters, metal-workers, and people working in leather and cloth. Such people provided a variety of plates, dishes, religious objects, decorative metal-work, tools, clothes and shoes – all of which will have had a constant and steady demand. Special items, such as samian ware imported from Gaul, will have been brought in by itinerant traders, and then sold in shops in the civilian settlements. However, at none of the civilian settlements outside the forts of the Lune valley have such activities as yet been positively recognised and located, although their products obviously feature in the site-finds.

The only industrial sites which have been definitely recognised are those at Quernmore, some three miles to the south-east of Lancaster.[15] At two sites, separated by approximately three miles, kilns have been located which were manufacturing floor-bricks and

44. The firemouth of the Roman tile-kiln excavated at Low Pleasant, Quernmore, in 1971.

roofing-tiles as well as a wide range of pottery vessels. There was some evidence at one of the sites of metal-working also. The discovery of roofing-tiles and bricks stamped by the cavalry-unit at Lancaster, the *Ala Sebosiana*, makes it clear that these sites had an official status, inviting a comparison with sites elsewhere, such as Holt in Denbighshire.[16] The sites at Quernmore appear to have been operating from *c.*A.D. 80 to *c.*A.D. 150; the termination of activity probably coincided with the enhanced organisation of manufacture and supply for the military market, which is evident from the earlier years of the second century A.D. with the inception of sites such as Wilderspool and Walton-le-Dale and with the introduction of

45. Typical pottery from the Quernmore kilns. (Lancaster City Museums.)

mass-production of such pottery-types as black-burnished ware and Nene Valley ware. It is also worth noting that whilst much of the tile found at Lancaster can be linked by trace-analysis to production at Quernmore,[17] voussoir-tiles associated with the fort bath-house clearly originated from a quite different source. It is not clear whether Quernmore serviced Lancaster alone, or perhaps supplied Burrow-in-Lonsdale also.

We may be certain that Quernmore was not an isolated site and that other military industrial complexes await discovery in the Lune valley. It is also likely that other forms of industry remained outside the civilian settlements; some metal-workers may have preferred their traditional ways and remained outside the new settlements, following an ancient trade but now providing for a new market. Further, the manufacture of items from leather and wool may also have been carried out at the farms themselves, and not necessarily always based upon centralised settlements.

However, the development of such communities with their wide range of needs will also have led to an 'industry' based upon the acquisition of raw materials; we have already seen that building-stone for the fort at Low Borrow Bridge may have been brought over a considerable distance. Besides this trade, which the army itself may have organised, there was a need for such commodities as iron,[18]

46. Roman lime-kiln found at Low Pleasant, Quernmore, in 1970–71.

coal, limestone, potters' clay and the grit-stone required for the manufacture of querns. Nor should we forget the salt-industry, where the raw material may well have been acquired in the Lune estuary, and brought perhaps to Lancaster for processing.

The Rural Economy

Within the Lune valley, as elsewhere, the majority of people will have remained what their families had long been – arable farmers in the valley-floors and up to approximately 700 feet,[19] and stock-managers on the higher ground. Some undoubtedly continued to exploit nature by hunting deer and wild boar, trapping wild fowl, and, to judge from the discovery of salmon-bones at Lancaster, by fishing in the Lune and its tributaries. Already, in prehistory, some farmers – those who became tribal leaders – had progressed from a simple self-sufficiency to the production of a saleable surplus. It is evident that in the north-west, as elsewhere in Britain, some farmers became sufficiently wealthy to be able to take on certain functions of locally-devolved

47. This altar from Weardale records the killing of a wild boar, 'of exceptional size, which his predecessors had failed to catch', by C. Tetius Veturius Micianus, commander of the Ala Sebosiana. We cannot prove that the unit was in Lancaster at this date but it is nice to think of Micianus taking a few days off duty in order to hunt with brother officers from somewhere like Bowes or Brough. (P. Thompson.)

administration. Thus, we should not be trapped into believing in the north-western stereotype of a small rural population, pathetically struggling to stay alive. Before the Romans came, some were already prosperous and powerful; the opportunities offered by the occupation meant that many more followed in their footsteps.

Woodland-clearance was already underway in late prehistory, and the coming of the Romans with their extensive requirements for timber for building and for burning in such amenities as bath-houses will have greatly accelerated this process. A result of this was increased soil-erosion at higher altitudes and enhanced soil-fertility in the valley-floors. There cannot, however, have been *uncontrolled* removal of woodland, since this would not only have diminished the supply of this particular raw material, but also upset the ecological balance of the valley, destroying, for example, the habitats of those wild animals which, as we have seen, will have provided a source of livelihood for some. This presupposes the practice of some level of woodland-management, which may, for example, have lain behind the forestry-clearance noted in the fourth century in the hinterland of Lancaster.[20]

The land of the Lune valley will have been divided into the *territorium* of each fort; if, indeed, devolved government came into the valley in the third century, then the administration of these *territoria* will have become the jointly-held responsibility of military and civilian authorities. Otherwise, the writ of the fort-commanders will have run unchallenged through the valley.

The boundaries of the fort-*territoria* cannot easily be reconstructed, although natural boundaries, such as sizeable streams, will have played a part. Milestones possibly provided boundary-markers. At the time of occupation, each fort-commander will have decided on the usage of the land in his *territorium*; some, no doubt, was 'confiscated' for distribution to time-expired military veterans. This will probably have consisted mainly of the fertile land of the valley-floors; at Folly

48. An altar to the god Jalonus Contrebis from Folly Farm just to the north of Lancaster. It was dedicated by Julius Januarius, a retired cavalry officer, and probably stood on his farmland. (Photograph by G. Harris.)

Farm, one mile to the north of Lancaster, as we have seen, we have evidence of one such veteran, Julius Januarius, making a dedication – presumably for a fruitful harvest – to the god, Jalonus, who was possibly the presiding deity of the river Lune.[21] The invocation of a local deity by this ex-soldier is indicative of the degree of his local commitment at a period which the style of the inscription would place in the late second or early third centuries. No evidence has been found of Januarius' farm itself, although the overall burden of evidence would suggest that it is unlikely to have been easily distinguishable from native farmsteads. Despite unverified rumours of mosaic pavements – for example, at Hornby and Brookhouse – there is no evidence at all for Romanised villas in the Lune valley. The 'pavement' recorded at Hornby was, in fact, clearly medieval in date.

Some land may have been appropriated for the direct use of the

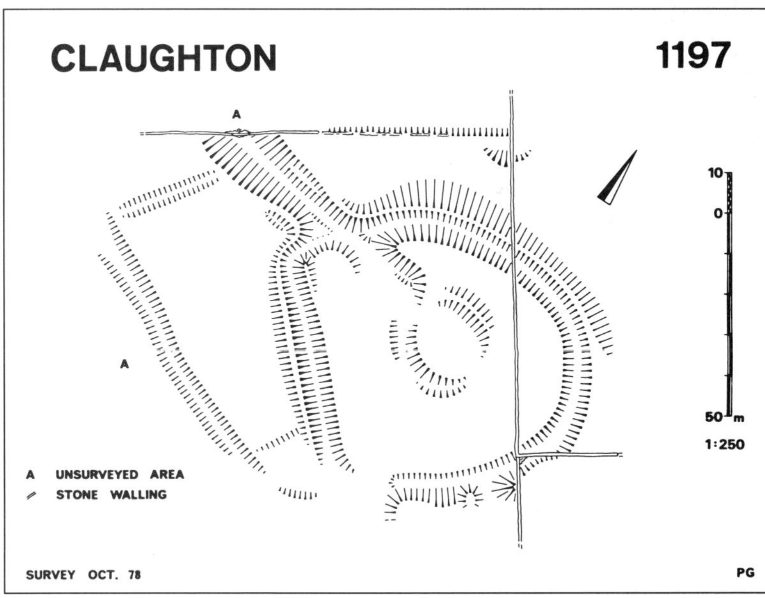

49. Aerial photograph of a farmstead at Claughton looking south west and plan. The earthworks are at the centre of the picture; Claughton Hall is to the left and the village of Claughton is to the top right. (Photograph by A. C. H. Olivier; plan by Paul Gibbons; courtesy of Lancaster University Archaeological Unit.)

garrisons themselves; there may have been a tendency for this to happen in the close vicinity of forts whose garrisons consisted wholly or partly of cavalry, for it will have been particularly convenient to have had supplies of fodder and bedding at hand; analysis of the material recovered in 1973 from a timber-lined well [22] close to the east gate of the fort at Lancaster emphasises the large-scale need

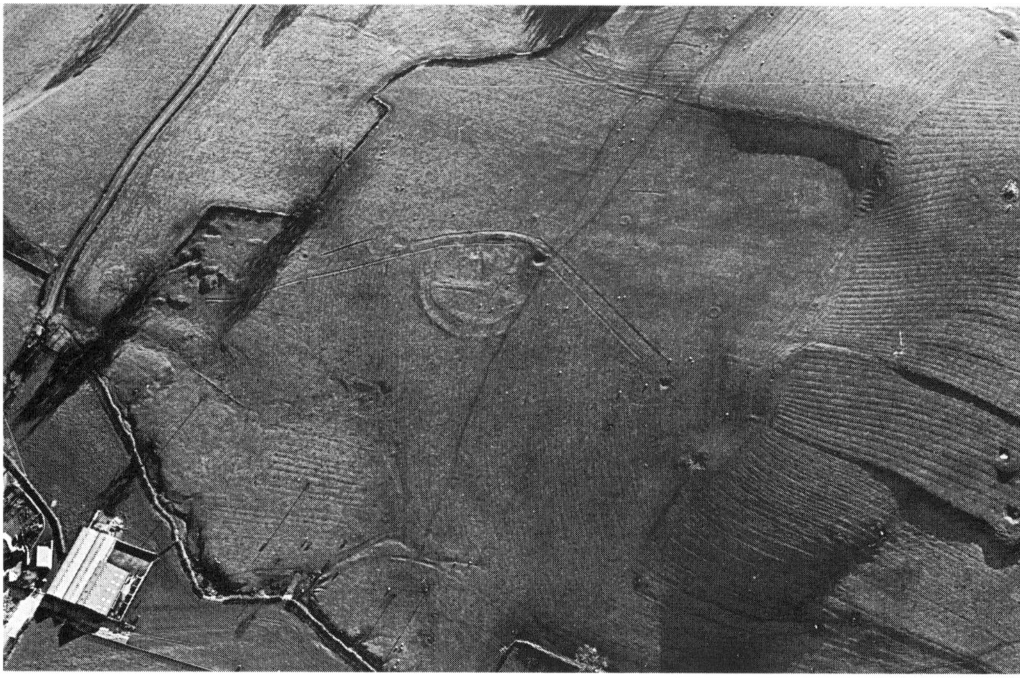

50. Aerial photograph of a farmstead at Sellet Hall near Whittington, looking south. It is in the form of a circular banked enclosure. The smaller circular earthworks are later coal-pits. (Photograph by A. C. H. Olivier, courtesy of Lancaster University Archaeological Unit.)

for hay for horses' fodder and bedding. This may have been supplied locally, though the organisation by the army of 'bulk-supplies' remains a possibility.[23] It is worth noting, however, that pollen-analysis [24] has indicated extensive pastoralism in southern Lakeland and at Cockerham Moss, the latter of which will certainly have fallen within the *territorium* of the fort at Lancaster.

The bulk of the land-organisation in each fort-*territorium*, however, probably left existing farmers largely undisturbed – either as continuing owners or as tenants of Rome, if the land concerned had been formally appropriated. In general, the Roman authorities were pragmatists, believing firmly in the principle that local people knew best how to exploit local conditions.

Field-work to elucidate features of the rural landscape has proceeded patchily, although most attention has so far been given to the upper and middle reaches of the Lune valley.[25] The lower reaches,[26] as the valley widens towards the estuary, have been subject to more long-term and extensive ploughing, which has caused severe damage to, even obliterated, such fragile sites. Thus, whilst a great density of sites is recorded in the area around Crosby Ravensworth and Crosby Garrett, between the head-waters of the Eden and the Lune, and again in the fells around Leck Beck and Eller Beck, only occasional sites are recorded in places such as Cantsfield, Arkholme and Halton. This should not, therefore, be taken as a true reflection of the landscape of the valley in the Roman period. Building-materials also contribute to the question of site-survival; in the valley itself, most sites consisted of a nucleus of sub-circular and sub-rectangular structures, built of timber and turf. From these nuclei radiate networks of the mostly small fields of the arable farmer. Above about eight hundred feet, the sites themselves, which may differ little in type, were constructed mostly of stone, and were the centres of systems of the much larger fields required for stock-ranching. All of these sites are notoriously difficult to date, as neither shape nor building-material appears to have much relevance to the problem. Indeed, many such sites go back in date well beyond the Roman period, thus prompting the suggestion that for some of them the period of the Roman occupation may not have been much more than an 'interlude'.[27]

There is wide variation in size amongst recorded sites; many are essentially small farmsteads, presumably for a single family-group, whilst others, such as Ewe Close (at Crosby Ravensworth) are so extensive that they have sometimes been thought of as 'villages' rather than farms. The difference in size, however, may be no more than a reflection of the simple, but important, difference between success and failure. Agricultural success in the north-west appears to be confirmed by the establishment in the third century A.D. of the *Civitas Carvetiorum*, for this presupposes the existence of people commanding sufficient wealth to perform the tasks in the community which were normally expected of *civitas*-leaders. It should be noted that the *civitas* of the Carvetii *may* have extended as far south as the northern end of the Lune valley. Of course, some of the larger (and more successful) farms may have belonged to discharged veterans of the Roman army who presumably enjoyed resources superior to those available to many of their local counterparts. Find-spots of Roman coin-hoards or even single coins,[28] for example, the gold *solidus* of the emperor, Valens (A.D. 364–78), which was found some three miles south of the fort at Low Borrow Bridge – *may* point to a farm nearby which belonged to such a veteran.

Farmers of all kinds will, of course, have found success by 'catering' for the markets which the Roman forts and their associated civilian settlements represented. This will have meant not just grain-crops and meat for human consumption, but, as we have seen, animal-fodder also. There were the by-products, too, such as leather and skins for clothes and tents. In the somewhat better climate which apparently prevailed in the second and third centuries, the area may have seen the provision of some specialist crops, such as vines. The Vindolanda-tablets offer a glimpse of the working relationship between a fort and those who lived in its hinterland.

The civilian settlements outside forts were usually small in overall extent, giving way rapidly to a 'suburbia' of small farms. Those farmers who lived in such close proximity to the main centres of population – for example, at Low and High Carlingill, just south of

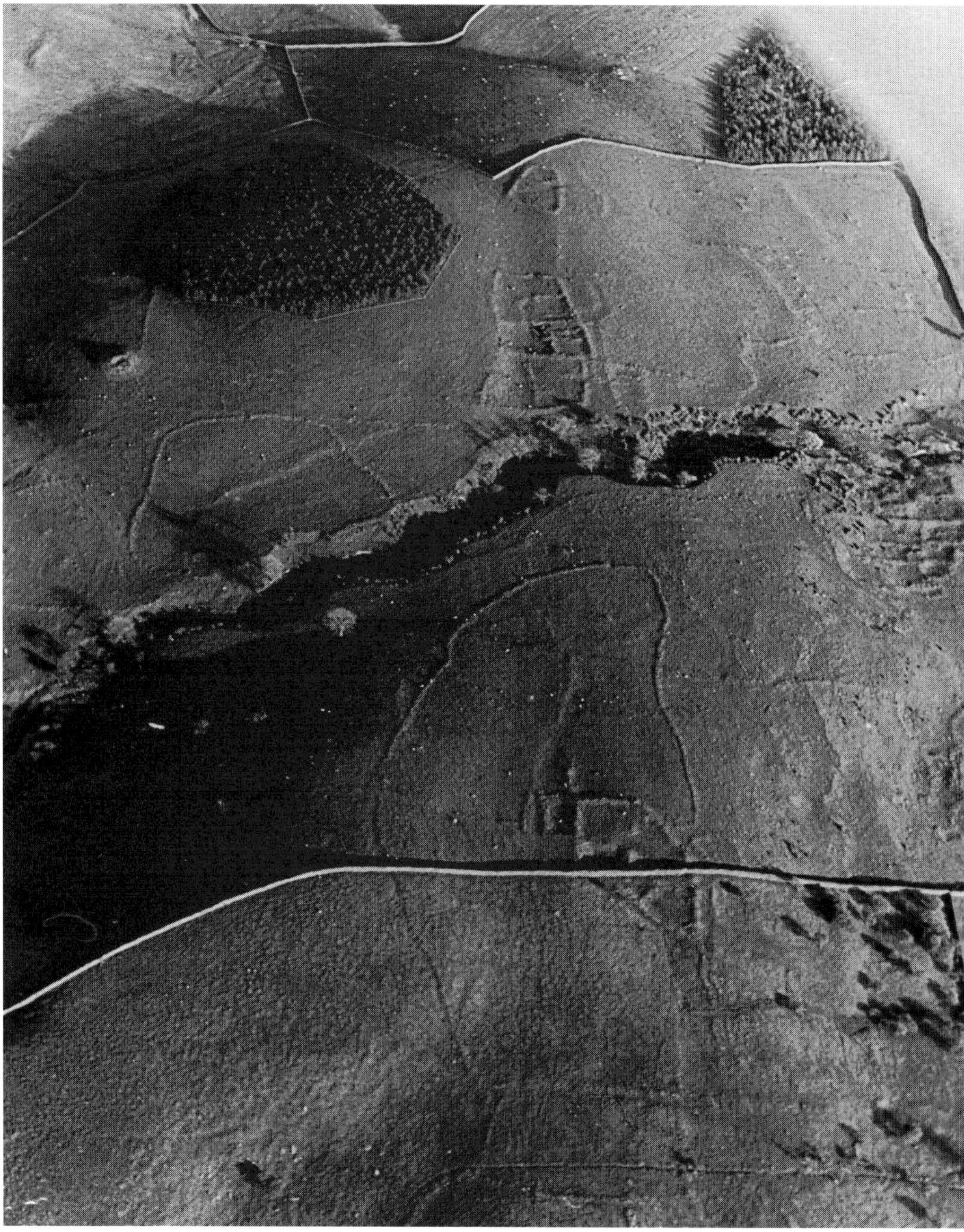

51. At Eller Beck, near Tunstall, the traces of ancient farmsteads and fields extend for long distances, relatively undisturbed. This landscape does not appear to have been ploughed in centuries. (Photograph by courtesy of G. D. B. Jones/Manunair.)

52. At Middleton are earthworks of what seems to be a small sub-rectangular farmstead and beside it what may be a circular Roman signal station. Neither has been excavated. (Photograph by courtesy of G. D. B. Jones/Manunair.)

the fort at Low Borrow Bridge – obviously had the opportunity to study the market and thus provide for it more precisely. Studies [29] of the bones of ox, sheep and pig from archaeological sites may point to the choice of an optimum age of slaughter for the meat-trade; this, in its turn, suggests the existence of 'arrangements' between individual farmers and the fort-authorities, or perhaps with individual traders within the civilian settlements, who will have received 'on the hoof' animals designated for slaughter.

Thus, although the picture of the rural population is far from perfect, enough survives to suggest that in time a relationship developed between forts, civilian settlements and farmers that was not only harmonious, but mutually profitable too. Some, however, remained marginal to this success-story; for every society has its 'under-class'. Some may have ended up as slaves in the households of those whose status and wealth encouraged them to enjoy this symbol of their position; others may have been beggars in the streets of the civilian settlements; others still, perhaps, lived out a life of brigandage in hideaways such as Dog Hole cave on the Iron-Age hillfort at Warton Crag (near Carnforth). This 'under-class' was in its own way as much as symbol of the prosperity of the Roman occupation as those who profited from it in a more orderly and conventional fashion.

Places to Visit

Roads: many stretches of Roman road are visible in the landscape of the present day – for example, through Barbondale and north and south of the fort at Low Borrow Bridge. The Middleton milestone may still be seen in a field to the west of the modern road (A 683) between Casterton and Sedbergh, although there is *no right of access* to it. The Caton milestone is in Lancaster City Museum.

Industry: the sites at Quernmore are not visible, though finds from them, including a fragment of roof-tile stamped by the *Ala Sebosiana* and found in the eighteenth century, are in Lancaster City Museum.

Farms: those farm-sites which survive in the landscape are best seen from the air, and are very hard to interpret on the ground. However, substantial remains survive around Crosby Ravensworth, at Low Carlingill (near Low Borrow Bridge), in the region of Eller Beck, and near Cantsfield. The Sites and Monuments Registers at Lancaster University and at County Hall, Kendal, can provide information on known sites. Such finds as there are from such sites are in Lancaster and Kendal Museums.

Notes to Chapter 6

1. *RIB* 601.
2. Shotter and White, 1990, 47–50.
3. *RIB* 2272.
4. Charlesworth, 1965, 427.
5. Birley, 1953.
6. See below for sections dug across this road; see also, Graystone, 1992.
7. See *Contrebis* II (1974), 51–2 (Holme Fell); Higham and Jones, 1985, 51 (Middleton Hall).
8. Most recently by T. M. Allan in a note published in Newsletter No. 4 (Spring 1985) of the Cumberland and Westmorland Antiquarian and Archaeological Society. We are grateful to Dr. Allan for a sight of his full notes on this section of road.
9. See *Britannia* XXIII (1992), 272.
10. Margary, 1973, 377ff
11. Edwards, 1977, 64–5
12. Ewbank, 1960, 28–31
13. Macadam, 1964, 76–80
14. As has been clearly demonstrated in the case of Manchester (Jones, 1974).
15. Jones and Shotter, 1988, 84–93.
16. See Grimes, 1930.
17. See *Contrebis* III (1975), 50–2.
18. Penney, 1983.
19. Higham, 1986, 117–49.
20. Oldfield and Statham, 1964–5.
21. *RIB* 600.
22. Jones and Shotter, 1988, 170–8.
23. Manning, 1975.
24. Oldfield and Statham, 1964–5.
25. For the upper reaches of the valley, see in particular Higham and Jones, 1975 and 1985; Higham, 1979 and 1980. For the middle reaches, see Lowndes, 1963 and 1964. A considerable number of sites, which have been long-known, are listed in *RCHM* (Westmorland).
26. Some sites in the lower reaches of the Lune are described in Howard-Davis, 1983–4, 3–25; for Cantsfield, see Shotter and White, 1990, 55.
27. Higham, 1986, 182ff.
28. Shotter, 1990.
29. Jones and Shotter, 1988, 167–9; Jones, 1975, 93–106.

Chapter 7

The Later Years

The Roman world of the fourth century A.D. was a very different place from that of early imperial times and had more in common in some ways with that of the Middle Ages. This period has been least studied and least understood by students of Roman Britain. Of the large number of significant changes which occurred between the second and fourth centuries we shall examine just four which seem to have a bearing upon our area.

Christianity, which had been a relatively minor and submerged force in the first and second centuries, gradually developed and spread throughout the Roman world. In A.D. 312 the Emperor Constantine gave it the status of not only the official religion of the Empire but of the *only* official religion, a far cry from the previous policy of tolerating a wide range of cults. This reflected the growing strength and organisation of the Christian church; at the Council of Arles in A.D. 314 there were many bishops present including three from Britain alone. Clearly such organisation could not have emerged, as it were, overnight.

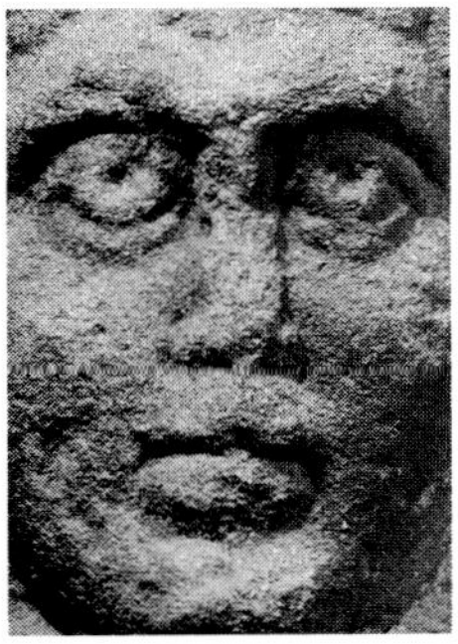

53. Detail from one of the statues found at Deep Cutting on the line of the Lancaster Canal in 1794. (Lancaster City Museums.)

In our area there is as yet no direct evidence for Roman Christianity. A lamp in Lancaster City Museum bearing a chi-rho ('Christos') symbol, which is often put forward as evidence for early Christianity in the area, is unfortunately without provenance and may well be of north African origin. Some have seen the deliberate burial of what seem to be funerary or cult statues at Deep Cutting on the south side of Lancaster, found during the digging of the Lancaster Canal, as evidence that the owners feared their desecration by Christians. Temples of Mithras on Hadrian's Wall, such as that at Carrawburgh, show signs of being levelled at this time, perhaps as a mark of official disfavour.

There is also the matter of the alignment of the Norman Priory in Lancaster with internal structures and roads of the Roman fort. This may indicate that religious use of the site is very early, while enough of the fort still stood to influence its alignment, but just how early is not clear. Most probably the Christian church came to occupy the site in the immediate post-Roman period, rather than in the fourth century. This question is complicated by the fact that the church is aligned with the fort of the first-to-third centuries and not with its fourth-century successor, which seems to have been radically re-aligned. Problems such as this remain to be resolved by future excavation.

The Roman army saw many changes, particularly under the reforms of the emperors Diocletian and Constantine. While historians have exaggerated the importance of some of these reforms there is no doubt that the army was henceforth divided into *limitanei* (garrison-troops), protecting key frontiers, and the *comitatus* (mobile armies), able to withstand and cope with rapidly-changing situations and threats. The mobile armies tended to become an elite, with the best troops and equipment. They also demonstrate graphically the growing barbarisation of the army; fierce barbarian troops such as the Herules were brought within the Roman empire and set to defend it against their even more barbarous cousins. Partly this was due to the always-overstretched nature of the imperial frontiers, which was itself due to an increasing shortage of manpower.

We should expect to find garrisons in the forts of Lunesdale at this time to be smaller and less centrally controlled. Changes in the army tend to be reflected in the looser layout of forts with a tendency for barrack blocks to become a series of 'chalets' and for stores and workshops to invade what had once been administrative or living accommodation – such is the evidence from Hadrian's Wall. This was accompanied by a change in building methods. It has been observed in a number of recent excavations on forts such as Rudchester and Ravenglass that stylobate construction becomes common in the fourth century.[1] So, instead of earth-fast timber or solid stone construction, we now find timber buildings set on padstones or with their uprights set in stone sockets. Gates were reduced in size and some blocked altogether. Non-standard buildings in unusual locations, such as the one inserted into the south gate at Burrow, frequently prove to be significant in late Roman contexts.

In recent years techniques of archaeology have improved greatly, allowing archaeologists to recognise very lightly-constructed buildings of the fourth century and possibly later which were previously either not recognised or missed altogether. This constructional evidence is particularly important because coins and pottery become notably scarce and die out altogether around A.D. 400, if not before; so there is a quantitative change in material evidence as well as a qualitative one after about A.D. 370.

Along with changes within the forts seems to go a loss of civilian settlements. At one time it was thought that civilians took up residence within the forts, but it does not appear likely that the traditional discipline and structure of the army had yet fallen to the point of it becoming a citizen-militia. Indeed, recent opinion has been in favour of it being remarkably unchanged except in status and details of tactics and armour. More work on civilian settlements needs to be done in order to establish the truth, but the truth is likely to be more complicated and variable from site to site than we at present think.

Some forts were not simply rebuilt on slightly modified plans but were wholly reconstructed to embody new principles of defence,

54. This great mass of mortared stonework was all that was visible of Roman Lancaster until 1973. It is all that is left of the Wery Wall, the massive fourth-century fort wall seen by earlier antiquaries.

such as were being tried on the Rhine and Danube frontiers.[2] At Lancaster, as we have seen, the earlier fort seems to have been levelled and the courtyard building to the north with its bath suite was demolished and replaced in about A.D. 340 by a deep ditch and a massive new stone curtain wall, the last relic of which is known as the 'Wery Wall', probably from the Anglo-Saxon *werian*, 'to defend'.[3]

This new fort, of which only two sides can at present be located, was of a type familiar from the south and east coasts of England and the northern coast of France. New forts in this area are associated with the so-called 'Saxon Shore' and represent the response to a new threat from raiders and settlers from what are now Holland, Germany and Denmark.

Lancaster's new fort seems to date from about A.D. 340 and so was somewhat later than the Saxon Shore forts, which originated in the last years of the third century. It may be associated with other west-coast sites like Cardiff, Caer Gybi in Holyhead and the mysterious Hen Waliau in Caernarfon, all of which have thick high walls and are probably connected with joint army and fleet activities against pirates in the Irish Sea. The threat may have been different from that of southern and eastern England but the response was much the same, reflecting the most up-to-date tactical thinking. The new fort at Lancaster seems to indicate not only great strategic importance for this site but also some economic significance for its region – the cost of fortifications such as this had to be justified.

Alongside changes in religion and the army came changes in

55. During excavations in 1973 the Wery Wall was excavated and the later garden wall crowning it was removed. It proved to be part of a corner bastion for the fourth-century fort. The stones in the foreground represent the base of the wall, all the rest having been robbed away.

56. The wall and bastion of the late-Roman fort at Caer Gybi, Holyhead. This may have been similar to the fort at Lancaster, but the walls have survived almost complete.

administration. Britain ceased to be a single province in 197 and was divided first into two, then into four under Diocletian, and perhaps five in about 370 [4] forming the *diocese* of *Britanniae* or 'the Britains'. This may have had little effect on ordinary people but it no doubt led to regional variations and to the rise of certain towns as provincial capitals. Very little evidence survives as to how the new arrangements worked in practice. The late Roman world became more bureaucratic and power was divided among many officials – perhaps intended to remove the temptation for an unscrupulous provincial governor to make a fortune through the concentration of power in his hands. Ranks in society continued on the whole to match the ancient division into patricians and plebs but a new rank of *viri clarissimi* represented what had once been called *equites* or knights, wealthy career-minded men, not of patrician stock, who had increasingly taken over the running of the empire as soldiers and administrators.

Public service to towns and other local communities as magistrates or officials had become increasingly onerous and expensive, to the point where large-scale avoidance set in. This may in part explain why it became fashionable and desirable in the fourth century for the wealthy to live upon their large country estates which for centuries they had been content to have run for them by bailiffs. This led to a late flowering of villas with new buildings, polychrome mosaics and wall-paintings. In the same context it is of interest to note that pollen-analysis from Cockerham Moss and the southern Lake District demonstrates extensive pastoral activity in the late Roman period with some arable, followed later on by forest regeneration.[5]

Many features point to the fourth century as being a time of hope, prosperity and culture, far removed from the old ideas of decline and fall. But time was running out for the western empire. Central control from Rome or Ravenna was becoming increasingly precarious and several times in the last years of the century was entirely dislocated by rebellion. It used to be thought that Honorius' letter to the *civitates* in A.D. 410 was an official relaxation of the *lex Iulia* forbidding citizens to carry arms and represented the end of centralised Roman rule in Britain. This contrasts somewhat with the historical evidence from the historian, Zosimus, which suggests that by 410 Britain was out of touch with Rome through the activities of the usurper Constantine III. It now appears that Honorius' letter was not after all addressed to Britain. We must therefore envisage no sudden end to Roman rule but rather a series of interruptions after which central control became irrelevant.

It is certainly a mistake to envisage Roman soldiers marching back to Rome. For many generations now they had been rooted in their provinces; they had nothing to do with Rome. Their remaining leaders probably became hereditary chieftains or warlords and the troops a sort of militia or war-band, until the last relics of Roman civilisation were a dim memory. In some areas subject to early invasion and settlement Roman life may have broken down quite soon whereas other areas may have retained vestiges of Roman civilisation much longer. North Lancashire was not settled by Germanic peoples at all until about A.D. 580 at the earliest, while the Lake District was hardly affected by these peoples; both are likely to have enjoyed a long period of sub-Roman Celtic civilisation. Nonetheless there is so far a total absence of the types of archaeological evidence we have now come to expect for places occupied within this sub-Roman phase.

This evidence is represented by several types of artefact, such as Phocaean Red Slip Ware pottery from western Turkey, similar wares from north Africa and also heavily ribbed amphorae from various parts of the eastern Mediterranean, including Greece.[6] It also exists in the form of memorial stones, giving the name of the deceased and sometimes other incidental information, in debased Roman lettering, ogham script, or sometimes both.[7] These occur widely in Wales, the west country and southern Scotland. Both types of evidence come from sites of chieftainly power and from monasteries; Christianity may be the important link. Western seaways remained open to saints and missionaries and perhaps merchants between the Mediterranean world and Atlantic Britain long after the fall of Rome.[8]

Red Slip Ware and sherds of ribbed amphorae *have* been found in Lancaster,[9] but neither from certainly post-Roman contexts. Perhaps the evidence has just not yet been found. Roman forts are likely to be fruitful sources of new information since in the north they, not towns, had always been the means of Romanisation. Birdoswald fort on Hadrian's Wall is yielding structural evidence for early post- Roman activity, and, as we suggest above, Burrow-in-Lonsdale may have similar things to show. Low Borrow Bridge is in a remote area where sub-Roman culture may have lingered long; 'Castlehows' may not be an entirely backward-looking name but may reflect some warlike tradition about the place.

Notes to Chapter 7

1. Breeze and Dobson, 1978, 222–4
2. von Petrikovits, 1971
3. White, 1976, 24
4. It has been suggested that *Valentia* was not a fifth province of Britain but actually a renaming of Britain itself, in honour of Valentinian; see Johnson, 1980, 98
5. Oldfield and Statham, 1964–5, 1–16
6. Thomas, 1959, 89–111; Fulford, 1989, 1–6
7. Nash-Williams, 1950
8. Bowen, 1972, 70–91
9. Bird, 1977, 275

Chapter 8

Conclusion

Even such a venerable subject as Roman history does not stand still. Apart from excavations which can reveal fresh and unsuspected structural evidence there are new interpretations and syntheses and new scientific approaches, not to mention whole new classes of material which can be made to yield their quota. While the pace of excavation has greatly reduced in recent years, mainly because of tighter funding and a recession in the large-scale building developments which made it necessary, advances have been rapid in other fields.

One of the biggest casualties of new interpretation has been the almost total collapse of the unified chronology based on Hadrian's Wall ('Wall-periods') which had been extended gradually to cover many other sites in the northern military zone. It is clear that no longer can we confidently ascribe widespread destruction, abandonment or rebuilding to one of a set series of historical events. Rather we must now assume that each site has its own unique chronology, with more or less constant patching, remodelling and rebuilding, and that different parts of the same site may even have a different history due to partial use, partial change or partial abandonment. This means that the theory that a whole series of truths can be established from a small sample-excavation is no longer tenable, and this in turn throws doubt upon many of the conclusions reached through such methods in the past.

Improvements in remote sensing, such as the use of gradiometers, magnetometers and ground radar, give hope that much may be learned about a site without disturbing the ground at all, or that excavation can be limited to resolving particular cruxes revealed by these methods.

One very important development of recent years has been the discovery of large deposits of Roman writing-tablets. While these are so far limited to sites with suitably damp environments to preserve these slivers of wood, the information derived from them provides new information in two ways. The first is that correspondence found at a fort like *Vindolanda*/Chesterholm relates not only to that fort but to garrisons all over the north of England. Hence the *Ala Sebosiana* has at last emerged on a writing-tablet from Carlisle, another 'wet' and potentially productive site for such material.[1] The second, and more important, benefit is that the kind of information revealed by these tablets is different from and complementary to that derived from official inscriptions. It provides a view of the private and unofficial world – sometimes perhaps of reality, when we consider that these letters reveal that garrisons were consistently under strength through sickness and detachment of units to serve elsewhere, something which was guessed at hitherto, but unprovable.[2]

Notes to Chapter 8

1. *Tab. Luguv.* 19; see I. D. Caruana, *The Roman Forts at Carlisle; Excavations at Annetwell Street, 1973–84*, (forthcoming)
2. Birley, R., 1989, 275

Appendix I

Portus Setantiorum

A NOTE is appropriate in the present volume on two problems, which, though usually linked, are not necessarily related: these are the location of *Portus Setantiorum*, and the likelihood of a Roman site in the vicinity of Fleetwood, perhaps lost by centuries of coastal erosion.

Of the authenticity of *Portus Setantiorum* ('The Harbour of the Setantii') there is little doubt. Although mentioned only by the geographer, Ptolemy of Alexandria,[1] its location in the north of Britain can be regarded as reliable; further, if Ptolemy's location is correctly transmitted, then its place in the north-west seems assured. The name itself highlights two problems: where was there a harbour *of significance*, since few recorded place-names in Roman Britain contain the *Portus*-element? Secondly, where was the territory of the Setantii located, a tribal group that is not otherwise attested?

Although northern England is generally regarded as the territory of the Brigantes, it is increasingly clear that other groups have to be accommodated.[2] It is, of course, unclear what degree of autonomy these may have achieved in the pre-Roman period, although some obviously did enjoy a measure of independence in the provincial arrangements – for example, the Carvetii of northern Cumbria.[3] In view, however, of the large area of territory apparently belonging to the Brigantes, it is difficult to believe that the writ of their monarch can have run effectively on an everyday-basis in all parts of the north; a certain amount of control must in practice have been 'devolved' to local leaders.

We should naturally expect that some indications would have survived of the status of a group capable of independent action; this produces a major impediment to accepting a location in the Fylde; for although the area has produced plentiful evidence of pre-Roman activity,[4] there is nothing in the record of topographical or artefactual observations to suggest sites of 'status-significance'. In other words, the area has no obvious tribal-centre. We should thus have to conclude that, even if the Fylde did belong to the Setantii, their chief centres were located elsewhere.

It has indeed been recently suggested [5] that the centres of gravity of the Setantii lay further to the north; their major sites may have been located at places such as Lancaster, Warton Crag, Skelmore Heads, and perhaps even as far afield as Ingleborough. Indeed, a location for *Portus Setantiorum* has been placed by some observers at Lancaster, though the weight of other evidence appears to argue against this.[6]

If we ascribe to the Setantii land in the southern Cumbrian coastlands as well as in north Lancashire, then not only can a tribal identity be more easily envisaged, but the 'Harbour of the Setantii' could be a site (now lost) with a coastal location between Lancaster and Barrow. Alternatively, in view of the evident use of Lake Windermere as an important link in the chain of communications and transport, with a major site at its northern end at Ambleside,[7] there is a case for expecting an equivalent site at the southern end of the lake – perhaps in the region of Newby Bridge – and identifying it as *Portus Setantiorum*.[8]

However, even if there is no pressing case for locating *Portus Setantiorum* at or near Fleetwood, this does not preclude the presence of a site of some kind in that area. Indeed, a number of factors seem positively to support it. First, significant finds of Roman material have been made along the lower Wyre, and particularly near its mouth. Casual finds of Roman coins have been made on Stalmine Moss (on Kate's Pad), at Skippool and Poulton, as well as at Fleetwood itself; those from Fleetwood include some unusually early issues for north-west England.[9] More significant, perhaps, from the point of view of settlement in the area are two substantial hoards of Roman coins: in 1840, a large hoard of silver coins was found at Rossall.[10] Accounts of it have become confused over the years, for, although the early reports describe it as a hoard of early imperial *denarii*, the Harris Museum at Preston has in its collection in excess of 400 late imperial *siliquae* which purport to be the Rossall Hoard. It would appear that a confusion has occurred – unless, of course, Rossall has yielded *two* large hoards of imperial silver. Secondly, in 1926, a hoard of some 300–400 radiate copies of the third century was found on the other side of the estuary in the vicinity of Hackensall Hall.[11] It is also possible that another hoard, also of radiate copies, was found in the 1930s on Preesall Hill,[12] and yet another at Poulton-le-Fylde in the nineteenth century.[13]

Evidence of a structural nature is more controversial: considerable records of observations exist of a road (*Dane's Pad*), assumed to be of Roman origin, running from Ribchester to Kirkham, and from there apparently heading for Poulton-le-Fylde and Fleetwood.[14] There, in the 1830s, at a place called 'the Warren' was seen the 'abrupt and broken termination of a Roman road';[15] the assumption made at the time was that this road was making for a location which is now offshore. Another track (or road), named *Kate's Pad* and constructed of timber, has long been known crossing Stalmine Moss.[16]

Coastal change in this area of the Fylde is well-attested; in 1555, for example, a village named Singleton Thorp was completely washed away from Rossall Grange, and various subsequent erosions have been noted. There is, therefore, no impediment to the notion that a Roman site may have been lost in similar fashion. It has indeed long been held that the *Dane's Pad* road was heading for a site where the Wyre flowed into the Lune, now some two miles off Fleetwood. Further, there are fascinating reports of submerged structures off the coast, the most explicit being a typed report of the 1970s prepared by Mr Ken Edwards.[17] This describes a wall some forty yards long, which lies at approximately two feet below the water at low tide. On the landward side, there is little depth behind it, but on the seaward side there is a drop of about fifteen feet, and the sea-bottom is strewn with tumbled masonry.

There is, of course, no proof that this masonry is of Roman origin, but the account of it serves to keep alive the notion that there was originally another Roman site on the Lune, *below* Lancaster. The truth of this will probably never be known, nor whether or not this was the elusive site of Ptolemy's *Portus Setantiorum*.

Notes

1. Ptol. *Geog.* II. 3. 2.
2. Higham, 1986, 145ff.
3. Higham and Jones, 1985.
4. Huckerby, Wells and Middleton, 1992.
5. Higham, 1986, 147.
6. Watkin, 1883, 77f; cf Shotter, 1993, 105ff.
7. Leach, 1993.
8. Shotter, 1995, (forthcoming)
9. Shotter, 1990, 219ff.
10. Shotter, 1990, 153–4 and 169–72.
11. Shotter, 1978, 47ff.
12. Shotter, 1990, 160–1.
13. Shotter, 1990, 177.
14. Watkin, 1883, 73ff; Middleton, 1992, 7f.
15. Watkin, 1883, 76, quoting Porter's *History of the Fylde* (1876), p. 7.
16. Huckerby, Wells and Middleton, 1992. *Kate's Pad* is now known to date from the early Bronze Age and it does not do to place too much reliance on earlier antiquarian traditions which make all things Roman.
17. This document is in the Lancashire Record Office at Preston.

Appendix II

List of selected dates

A.D.	
40s	Establishment of a treaty between Rome and queen Cartimandua of the Brigantes
60s	Temporary military intervention necessary in the north-west; Roman civil war; Cartimandua ousted by Venutius
71–4	Governorship of Petillius Cerialis; campaign in north-west England
77–83	Agricola in Britain
78	Campaign in north-west England
*c.*87	Withdrawal from Scotland to the Stanegate-frontier
*c.*102	Stone fort built at Lancaster
*c.*115–7	Disturbances in northern England
122	Building of Hadrian's Wall started
*c.*142–65	Antonine Wall; loss of garrison at Lancaster
*c.*215	Caracalla's treaty with the Scots; Lancaster demilitarised (?)
259–73	Breakaway-movement of the *Imperium Galliarum*
262	Bath-house at Lancaster re-dedicated
287–96	Rebellion of Carausius
296–306	Refurbishment of the northern frontier-area
312	Constantine's victory over Maxentius; acceptance of Christianity (edict of Milan)
*c.*340	Building of the Wery-Wall fort at Lancaster
*c.*340–50	Abandonment of extra-mural settlement at Lancaster (?); relocation of civilians inside new fort (?)
351	Rebellion of Magnentius
367	'Conspiracy of the barbarians', followed by repairs to military installations
380–	Withdrawals of some troops, leaving localised militias to look after their own settlements

Appendix III

Inscriptions from Roman Sites in the Lune Valley

THE foregoing pages have made use of the evidence provided by the small body of epigraphic evidence from Roman sites in the Lune Valley; the purpose of the present appendix is to provide that evidence in full. Most of this evidence is now published in *The Roman Inscriptions of Britain* (*RIB*), but new inscriptions are published annually in the journal, *Britannia*.

I: *Inscriptions on Stone* (R. G. Collingwood and R. P. Wright, 1965)

II: (fascicule 1): *Instrumentum Domesticum* (S. S. Frere, M. Roxan, and R. S. O. Tomlin, 1990)

II: (fascicule 4): *Instrumentum Domesticum* (S. S. Frere and R. S. O. Tomlin, 1992)

Lancaster

a) Inscriptions on Stone

i) *RIB* 600 (Plate 57). This altar was found in 1802, beside the Lancaster/Kendal canal, south of Folly Farm (that is, approximately one mile to the north of Lancaster). It is dedicated to the god, *Ialonus Contrebis*, who was possibly a meadow-land divinity associated with the river Lune; the element, *Contrebis*, appears also on *RIB* 610 from Burrow-in-Lonsdale. Indeed, the name, *Ialonus*, may conceal a Roman name for the river Lune. The dedication was made by Julius Januarius, a retired NCO from a cavalry-unit, and on grounds of style the inscription is thought to belong to the late second or early third centuries. It is possible that the find-spot of the altar represents the location of a farm which Januarius was given after his discharge from military service, and its dedication may represent a thank-offering for a successful harvest.

DEO
IALONO
CONTRE (bi)
SANCT[I]SS[I]
MO IVLIV[S]
IANVARIVS

57. *RIB* 600, from Folly Farm. (Photograph by G. Harris.)

58. *RIB* 601, found at Halton in 1794. (Photograph by G. Harris.)

EM (eritus) EX DEC (urione)
V (otum) [S (olvit)]

'To the most holy god, Jalonus Contrebis, Julius Januarius, retired former decurion, fulfilled his vow.'

The altar is in Lancaster City Museum.

ii) *RIB* 601 (Plate 58). This altar, which is broken down its right-hand side, was found in 1794 in the churchyard at Halton-on-Lune, although it may be assumed to have derived from Lancaster. It is dedicated to the war-god, Mars, by Sabinus and his irregular Unit of Boatmen; its chief significance lies in introducing into the Lancaster-area a previously-unknown unit of the Roman army (see Shotter, 1973, 206).

DEO
MART[I]
SABINV[S]
P (rae) P (ositus) ET MILIT[ES]

59. *RIB* 602, found on the north side of Lancaster Castle in 1797.
(Photograph by G. Harris.)

60. *RIB* 604, found in 1863 in the Priory Church, Lancaster.
(Photograph by G. Harris.)

N (umeri) BARC (ariorum) S (ub) C (ura)
EIIVS PO[S] (uerunt)

'To the god, Mars, Sabinus, the commander, and the soldiers of the Unit of Boatmen under his command, set this up.'

The altar is in Lancaster City Museum.

iii) *RIB* 602 (Plate 59). This altar was found in 1797 on the north side of the castle. It is dedicated to the Romano-Celtic god, Mars Cocidius; the paralleling of a Roman deity with his nearest Celtic equivalent was common practice. *Cocidius*, presumably a war-god, has left evidence at a number of places in the north, although the chief centre of his cult appears to have been at Bewcastle in Cumbria, the Roman name of which was probably *Fanum Cocidi.* Lucius Vibenius, the dedicator, is described as *beneficiarius consularis*, which indicates a legionary soldier, seconded as an aide to the provincial governor's staff, probably to act in a regional supervisory capacity, perhaps with special responsibility for matters of taxation.

DEO
SANCTO MARTI
COCIDIO VIBENIVS
LVCIVS B (ene) F (iciarius) CO (n) S (ularis)
V (otum) S (olvit) L (ibens) M (erito)

'To the holy god, Mars Cocidius, Lucius Vibenius, the governor's aide, willingly and deservedly fulfilled his vow.'

The altar is in Adrian's Tower at Lancaster Castle.

iv) *RIB* 603. This altar is stated to have been found around 1811 in a garden adjoining Vicarage Fields (Watkin, 1883, 169f). Its text is too weathered to permit reconstruction. It seems very likely that it is the same altar as that listed as *RIB* 607, which was found in Lancaster in 1753, reported by Stukeley, but subsequently lost.

The altar is in Lancaster City Museum.

v) *RIB* 604 (plate 60). This is the top left-hand corner-fragment of a dedication – or building-stone, which was found in 1863 in the Priory Church, on Castle Hill. It is dedicated to the emperor, Trajan (A.D. 98–117), and presumably offers evidence that the fort (or part of it) was rebuilt in stone during that emperor's reign. Its find-spot would put it close to the presumed location of the fort's headquarters (*principia*).

IMP (eratori) NER (vae)
TRAIANO
AVG (usto) [GER (manico) DAC (ico)]
C[

'To the Emperor, Nerva Trajan Augustus Germanicus Dacicus . . .' (Reconstruction is unsafe beyond this point).

The dedication-stone is in Lancaster City Museum.

vi) *RIB* 605 (Plate 61). This dedication-stone was found in 1812 in a garden at the junction of Church Street and Bridge Lane; it is fully discussed in Jones and Shotter, 1988, 208ff. It records the repair and rebuilding of a bath-house and basilica, which had collapsed through old age – often, though not necessarily, euphemistic language for the result of enemy-action. The stone has been dated, on the basis of its erasures and because of the fact that the consuls to whom it refers are not otherwise known, to the period A.D. 262–266 during the breakaway *Imperium Galliarum* (Birley, 1936, 5).

61. *RIB* 605, found in 1812 at the junction of Church Street and Bridge Lane. (Photograph by G. Harris.)

[/////// OB] BALINEVM REFECT (um)
[ET] BASILICAM VETVSTATE CONLABSVM
A SOLO RESTITVTAM EQ (uitibus) ALAE SEBVSSIAN (ae)
/////// SVB OCTAVIO SABINO V (iro) C (larissimo)
PRAESIDE N (ostro) CVRANTE FLA (vio) AMMAV
SIO PRAEF (ecto) EQ (uitum) D (e) D (icata) XI KAL (endas)
SEPTEM (bres)
CENSORE II ET LIPIDO II CO (n) S (ulibus)

The first erasure represents the emperor's name and titles, whilst the second represents an adjectival form of his name given honorifically to the *Ala Sebosiana*.

'(For the emperor, Postumus . . .) on account of the bath-house rebuilt and the basilica restored from ground-level, having collapsed through age, for the cavalrymen of the *Ala Sebosiana* under the senator, Octavius Sabinus, our governor, and Flavius Ammausius, the prefect of cavalry: dedicated on August 22nd in the year when Censor and Lepidus were consuls, each for the second time'.

The bath-house referred to was situated outside the east gate of the fort, whilst the *basilica* was probably a *basilica equestris exercitatoria*, a drill-hall attached to the *principia* of cavalry-forts.

The dedication-stone is in Lancaster City Museum.

vii) *RIB* 606. This tombstone was found in Cheapside in 1772, and is now lost; its reading is based upon contemporary drawings (Watkin, 1883, 184; Edwards, 1971, 23ff), and its date is likely to have been early in the second century A.D. Apart from its find-spot, which possibly indicates a cemetery-area, the stone's chief significance is in its reference to an *Ala Augusta*, which presumably (though not necessarily) had a period of garrison-duty at Lancaster; like the *Ala Sebosiana*, it was a Gallic unit, which explains the presence in it of a man from Trier.

DIS MANI
BVS
L (ucius) IVL (ius) APOL
LINARIS TREVER AN (norum)
XXX EQ (ues) AL
AE AV[G]
H (ic) [S (itus) E (st)]

'Sacred to the gods of the underworld. Here lies Lucius Julius Apollinaris, from Trier, aged thirty years, a cavalryman in the *Ala Augusta*'.

62. Fragment of an inscription from New Quay Road, Lancaster, 1976.

viii) *RIB* 607 (see above on *RIB* 603).

ix) Plate 62. In March 1976, a fragment of an inscription was found in the disused rubbish-tip at the western end of New Quay Road; the stone probably came from one of the many sites in Lancaster, which were being redeveloped in the mid-nineteenth century (*Contrebis* IV (1976), 22f).

[. . . . . . .] I
[. . . . . . .] ELICI
[. . . . . . .] OPATRI

Interpretation on the basis of such a small fragment is unclear; it might be a tombstone to 'my father, Felix'. Alternatively, it has been restored as a commemorative stone, with elements of the imperial titulary [PIO] FELICI [AVG (usto) . . .] O PATRI [PATRIAE.

Such a collection of titles might suit the emperor Caracalla (A.D. 211–217; *Britannia* XVII (1986), 436).

The stone remains in the finder's possession.

Note: The inscription (*RIB* 608), recorded by Watkin (1883, 172) as being on 'the base of a pillar', is now seen, on the basis of recently rediscovered drawings, to have been on the base of a pipeclay statuette. The 'inscription' is probably a maker's mark – possibly that of Servandus of Cologne (Edwards, 1971, 25ff: see now *RIB* 2456. 8).

b) Inscriptions and Stamps on tiles and bricks (*RIB* 2465, 1–2)

The majority of known tile and brick stamps from Lancaster derived from the excavations of 1973 (Jones and Shotter, 1988, 186 ff). A group of five fragments contained portions of incuse stamps which would probably in full have read

ALSBVSA

(for *Ala Sebosiana*); these are paralleled by an unprovenanced fragment exhibited in 1752 to the Society of Antiquaries of London, and bearing the inscription

ALSB

(*CIL* VII 1240), which formed part of a tile-tomb, found in 1752, and reported to William Stukeley. (Lukis, 1883, 240–1).

A fragment, bearing part of a framed stamp

] BVSIA

was found in ditch-fill in 1973 near to the site of the east gate of the fort; it appears to derive from the same die as the survivor (now in Lancaster City Museum) of those found at Quernmore in 1774 (*CIL* VII 1233; Watkin, 1883, 175–7). The surviving specimen reads

ALE SEBVSIA

(for the *Ala Sebosiana*). Watkin indicates that evidence contemporary to the find of 1774 pointed to the existence of a number of different stamps; a very abraded example of a different stamp was found in Lancaster in 1974, reading

] ESE [. .] S [

(see *Contrebis* III (1975), 53).

It is notable that all of the surviving and recorded evidence from Lancaster concerning this army-unit uses the form *SEBVSIA (na)* or *SEBVSSIA (na),* although the 'proper' form, *SEBOSIANA*,

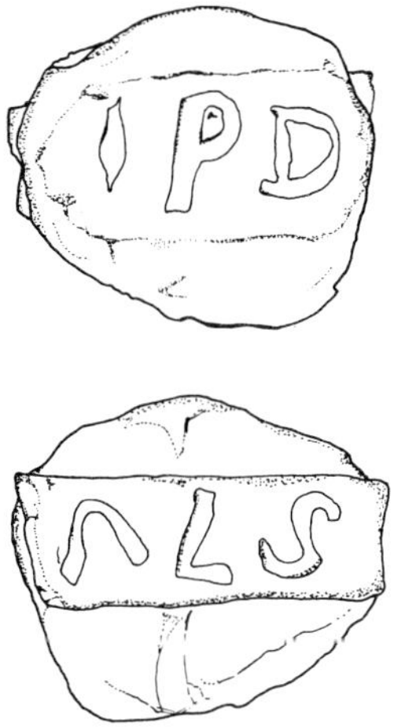

63. Lead sealing from Vicarage Field, Lancaster, 1973. (Lancaster City Mu-

appears on the Malpas Diploma (*CIL* XVI. 48; plate 11), on a tombstone from Mainz (*ILS* 2533; plate 18), and on the dedication to Silvanus from Bollihope Common in County Durham (*RIB* 1041; plate 47).

Two further pieces came from the excavations of 1973:
i) a brick-stamp, reading '] FEC (it)' – 'made this'.
ii) a brick bearing an alphabetic graffito, 'AB['

c) Lead sealing

(*RIB* 2411:88). This sealing was found on the Western Vicarage Field in 1973 (Jones and Shotter, 1988, 152). The sealing carried in relief the letters 'ALS' on the obverse face, and 'IPD' on the reverse. It seems likely that ALS stands for *Ala Sebosiana* whilst IPD conceals a personal name and rank. One of the large group of sealings from Brough-under-Stainmore had ALA SIIB on the obverse and VAL DEC on the reverse (Richmond, 1936, 120).
The sealing is in Lancaster City Museum.

Burrow-in-Lonsdale

i) *RIB* 610: (Plate 64) This altar was found built into one of the buildings at Burrow Hall and first recorded by Rauthmel in 1746. The simple inscription has caused many heartaches of interpretation but seems quite clearly to have been set up by someone – whether man or woman we cannot tell – with a Celtic name in honour of a god who also appears on *RIB* 600 from Folly Farm near Lancaster (see above). The god's name occurs only on these two inscriptions and appears to be Celtic. Whatever the etymology of the name the god is almost certainly the tutelary deity of the lower Lune valley.

DEO SAN (cto)
CONTR
EBI VAT
TA POSV (it)

'Vatta set this up to the holy god Contrebis.'

This altar is now lost.

64. *RIB* 610, found at Burrow Hall and illustrated by Rauthmel in 1746.

ii) *RIB* 613: Fragment of a red sandstone panel with a cable moulding at the top and two dowel-holes, found in 1951 outside the north-west corner of the fort.

]TTI M FIL
]VLLI PII

'. . . of ( ) uttius ( ) ullus Pius, son of Marcus . . .'

The inscription was at Burrow Hall in 1953 (Wright, 1954, 97), but is now lost.

iii) *RIB* 615: Fragment of buff sandstone from the bottom line of an inscription found in 1952 during excavation of the roadway at the south gate of the fort. It may represent part of an inscription mounted on the wall, or a stone reused in some later repair to the wall, or its position may be quite fortuitous.

]VIS[

RIB reads this as part of 'sit terra tibi levis' – 'may the earth lie light on thee' but this seems to us to be an unwarrantable extension to be based upon three letters. Perhaps one day another part of the inscription will turn up to throw light upon the full text.

The inscription was at Burrow Hall in 1953 (Wright, 1954, 97), but is now lost.

Low Borrow Bridge

Only two inscriptions are recorded from this site, both apparently tombstones.

i) *RIB* 756: This was seen before 1946 about one mile to the south of the fort in an area now known to have been occupied by a cemetery. It was re-used near the point of discovery to form the cover of a culvert, and has not been seen since. The description would suggest that it may have been the tombstone of a cavalryman, depicting a rider spearing a fallen enemy. The only portion of the inscription that was recalled by the finder was 'XX', which was presumably part of the age or length of service of a deceased soldier.

ii) (Plate 37): This was found in the excavation of 1991 on the site of the cemetery, one mile to the south of the fort. The text is inscribed in eight lines in letters of good quality, the stone was erected by Aurelius Verulus in memory of his wife, Aelia Sentica.

D (is) M (anibus)
AELIA SE
NTICA VI
XIT AN (nos) XXXV
AVREL (ius) VE

RVLUS CO
NIVGI KA
RISSIME.

'To the gods of the underworld: Aelia Sentica lived for thirty-five years. Aurelius Verulus set up this stone for his loving wife'.

A full discussion will appear in the forthcoming publication of the Low Borrow Bridge cemetery-excavation of 1991 (Lambert *et al.*, 1995).

Inscriptions from locations not recognised as Roman sites

a) Cockersand Moss

RIB 616, 617: In the Stukeley MSS in the Society of Antiquaries of London (MS 264 f8 and MS 265 f43) appears the following (the text is roughly the same in each case):

"There were found in Lancashire in Cockersand Moss Statues of Mars upon the Basis of the Greater is this Inscription

DEO MARTI NODONTI AVR
ELIVS______CINVS SIG

The Lesser Statue was of worse Age and make on one side

LVCIANVS at the End D___M____N

and on the otherside of the Pedistal

COL LIC APRILI VIATO At the End RIS VS

They were in my Lord Arundels Collection."

This can be translated as 'to the god Mars Nodons Aurelius ( )cinus set up this statue' and 'Lucianus fulfilled the vow of his colleague, Aprilis Viator, to the god Mars Nodons'.

The date of the note is *c.*1718 but it is not clear whether the two statues were still in Lord Arundel's possession at that time, nor when he had acquired them. It is possible that they were found much earlier and had come from the Dalton estates in Cockersand Moss (both the Dalton family and the Arundels were Catholic recusants and may have had contacts).

The present whereabouts of the statues is unknown, so the reference is all the more intriguing. They sound as if they were of bronze, like the famous Mars-statue from the Foss Dyke near Lincoln, but stone cannot be ruled out. Indeed, Katharine Eustace and Michael Vickers of the Ashmolean Museum, Oxford, (in litt.), suggest that the Arundel Cabinet contained mainly marble sculptures and that bronzes were mostly contemporary copies after the antique.

RIB lists four occurrences of inscriptions to Mars Nodens, so the identification of the two gods is by no means unique. Nodens was a Celtic god and a well-known temple dedicated to him was excavated at Lydney, in Gloucestershire, and seems to have been very late in date. While it is tempting to see a maritime link between Lydney (on the Severn estuary) and Cockersand Moss, there is no particular reason for assuming that these statues are late in the Roman period or evidence of cultural contacts. The equation with Mars suggests a military personification, rather than a healing one, so the Cockersand-statues may have been deposited by soldiers or sailors.

b) Kirkby Lonsdale

RIB 611: An altar to the deities of the emperor and the genius of the Guild of Apollo by Bellinus, recorded by Rev. Machell at Kirkby Lonsdale in 1684, is now lost (Ewbank, 1963, 24, 150). It was found in a bank at Abbot's Brow adjoining the north east side of the churchyard and was, when Machell saw it, lying in the High Street as a seat in front of 'Widdow Man's door'. The house known as Abbot's Brow is still there but the altar is no longer in the main street.

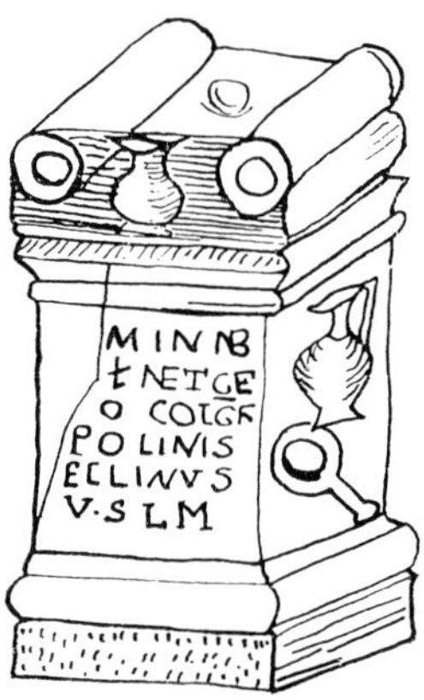

65. *RIB* 611, recorded at Kirkby Lonsdale in 1684 by Rev. Machell. (Reproduced by courtesy of the Council of the CWAAS.)

[NV]MINIB[VS]
[AV]G (usti) N (ostri) ET GE[N
I]O COLGF
[A]POLL[I]NIS
[B]ELLINVS
VSLM

'Bellinus willingly and deservedly fulfilled his vow to the spirits of our Emperor and to the genius of the Guild of Apollo"

This altar is now lost.

c) Tunstall

Fragments of three inscriptions have been recorded at Tunstall, all probably carried from Burrow in post-Roman times.

i) *RIB* 609: A small altar to Asclepius and Hygiaea set up by Julius Saturninus, now built into a window-sill on the north side of Tunstall church. The choice of such health-giving deities suggests that either the donor was a doctor or that he or a member of his family had recently had a serious illness. There is widespread evidence for doctors in the Roman army and Greek doctors were especially favoured. An inscription in Greek from Chester (Nutton, 1968, 7–13) is dedicated to the same deities, possibly joined by Panacaea. Perhaps Saturninus' origins prompted the choice of Greek deities and Greek forms of their names on this inscription; unfortunately his Romanised name renders his origins obscure.

66. This fragment of *RIB* 612 can still be seen in the wall of a roadside barn at Burrow.

DEO SANC[TO]
ASCLEP[I]O [ET]
HYGIAEAE [P (ro) S (alute) S]
VA CVM SV[IS]
IVL (ius) SATVRN (inus)

'Julius Saturninus (set this up) to the holy gods Asclepius and Hygiaea for the welfare of himself and his family'.

ii) *RIB* 612: *RIB* illustrates one fragment of this inscription but in 1967 by a brilliant piece of detective work B. J. N. Edwards was able to reconstruct one large gabled tombstone from two surviving fragments, including one newly discovered, and the drawing of the main fragment. This fragment itself has been lost for two centuries. When last seen in 1698 it was at the Vicarage in Tunstall, perhaps built into the wall (Ewbank, 1963, 150; Edwards, 1971, 17–34).

As reconstructed the inscription reads:

D
M S
ET PERPETVE SEC
VRITATI AVREVS (
) NNIO TV ( ) VIX
AN. LIIII MILI ( ) XXXVI
AVR EVBIAE CON ( ) EIIVS VIX
AN XXXVII AVRPP ( ) KARISSIM

'Sacred to the spirits of the departed and to the lasting calm of Aurelius Pusinnus, a citizen . . . who lived 54 years and had 36 years military service and of Aurelia Eubia his wife who lived 37 years. Aurelius Propinquus (or some such name) their beloved son (set this up)'.

While there are, not surprisingly, some technical problems in the restoration of this inscription there seems no doubt that it records a soldier and his wife from the fort at Burrow, and that their figures once appeared side by side in the niches beneath. His military service is greatly in excess of the usual twenty-five years but he seems to have joined the army at eighteen, which was quite normal. His wife was much younger than he was. Perhaps she was a child of the *vicus*?

One part of the tombstone, in red sandstone, is still to be seen in the wall of a barn next to the road at Burrow. Another fragment is now in Lancaster City Museum. The cable border to one of the niches is very plainly visible. This tombstone is quite the most elaborate yet found in Lunesdale and was probably of the free-standing house-shaped type, like those that lined the Appian Way outside Rome.

iii) *RIB* 614

Machell saw another fragment of a gabled tombstone at Tunstall Vicarage in 1698. It also had a pine cone and DMS in the gable and so perhaps came from a similar tomb. It is now lost.

Milestones

The Lancaster area has produced three milestones, all of which (i-iii) are in Lancaster City Museum.

i) *RIB* 2270. Found in 1811 at Burrow Heights, three miles south of Lancaster.

IMP (eratori) C (aesari) M (arco) IVLIO
PHILIPPO
PIO FEL (ici) AVG (usto)
N (ostro)

'For the Emperor Caesar Marcus Julius Philippus Pius Felix, our Augustus'. (A.D. 244–9).

ii) *RIB* 2271. Found in 1834, apparently close the the find-spot of RIB 2270.

IMP (eratori) C (aesari) D (omino) N (ostro)
GAIO MES[SIO]
QVINTO DECIO
TRAIANO PIO FEL
ICI INVICTO AVG

'For the Emperor Caesar, Our Lord, Gaius Messius Quintus Decius Traianus Pius Felix Invictus Augustus'. (A.D. 249–251).

67. *RIB* 2272, a milestone found in 1803 in the Artle Beck, Caton.

iii) *RIB* 2272 (Plate 67). Found in 1803 in the Artle Beck, at Caton.

IMP (eratori) CAES (ari)
TR (aiano) HA.D.RIANO
AVG (usto) P (ontifici) M (aximo) T (ribuniciae) P (otestatis)
CO (n) S (uli) III P (atri) P (atriae)
I L M (ilia) P (assuum) IIII

'For the Emperor Caesar Traianus Hadrianus Augustus, Chief Priest, Holder of Tribunician Power, Consul for the third time, Father of his Country. (From . . .) four miles'. (A.D. 127–138).

iv) At the sudden bend in the modern minor road between Burrow and Cowan Bridge, where the Roman road (Margary 7c) crosses it, the late Lord Temple recognised the stump of a Roman milestone in what is now a parish boundary marker. The cylindrical stump has no surviving Roman inscription (Charlesworth, 1965, 427). It lay beside the road from Ribchester to Low Borrow Bridge. The remaining stump is not inscribed. A roughly cylindrical piece of stone in a nearby garden was investigated by the second author in 1989 in the hope that it might be part of the same milestone. It proved negative, the stone not being bedded into the ground.

v) *RIB* 2283; (plate 40). The milestone is at Middleton-in-Lonsdale, where it now stands close to the A683 road; it was originally found in 1836 closer to the river, where, in the drought of early summer 1992, the road itself appeared as a parched linear feature. The significance of the milestone is fully discussed in Birley, 1953. A secondary inscription records its discovery and re-erection. The Roman inscription reads:

M (ilia) P (assuum) LIII

This is taken to indicate a distance of fifty-three miles, presumably from Carlisle.

The discovery of these milestones prompts speculation concerning their significance in the political and administrative landscape of the area. We cannot, of course, be certain of the frequency of disposition of milestones – whether they were erected at one-mile intervals, or whether they stood at points on the road-system that were significant.

It has been suggested, for example (Higham and Jones, 1985, 12), that the milestone at Middleton-in-Lonsdale, in recording a distance of fifty-three miles (evidently from Carlisle) indicates that the Upper Lune Valley came within the administrative competence of the tribe of the Carvetii, with their administrative centre at Carlisle. Whilst this is beyond proof, it may still be the case that milestones performed the important function of demarcating the *territorium* of individual forts.

Thus, the Middleton-milestone would mark a division between the *territoria* of Low Borrow Bridge and Burrow-in-Lonsdale, whilst the Caton-milestone might perform the same function between Burrow-in-Lonsdale and Lancaster. Similarly, the two milestones of the third century, found on the south side of Lancaster might denote something similar in that area. Clearly, however, this argument cannot be advanced too far, since the evidence does not survive for showing *territorium* – boundaries in other directions.

The *territorium* would obviously constitute a significant unit for the organisation of supplies to a fort; it might similarly be important for the mounting of patrols. In either case, the uneven *extent* of territory is obvious; in particular, the fort at Lancaster would on such an argument exercise a responsibility for less territory than either of the other two forts of the Lune Valley. In its turn, this might be related to the nature of the terrain and of the population, with the fort at Lancaster having less territory because in the lower reaches of the river the land was more densely populated, and thus more intensively utilised. The size of the *territorium* would thus be in inverse proportion to the intensity of its use (Higham and Jones, 1985, 105ff.).

Clearly, however, to pursue such an argument would require a great deal more evidence than currently exists.

Bibliography

Abbreviations:

Ant. J.	Antiquaries Journal
Arch. J.	Archaeological Journal
BAR	British Archaeological Reports
CBA	Council for British Archaeology
CIL	Corpus Inscriptionum Latinarum
CW	Transactions of the Cumberland and Westmorland Antiquarian and Archaeological Society
ILS	Inscriptiones Latinae Selectae
JRS	Journal of Roman Studies
LAB	Lancashire Archaeological Bulletin
LAJ	Lancashire Archaeological Journal
Med. Arch.	Medieval Archaeology
RCHM	Royal Commission for Historic Monuments
RIB	Roman Inscriptions of Britain

Alcock, 1965: Alcock J. P., Celtic Water-cults in Britain, *Arch. J.* CXXII, 1–12

Anstee, 1975a: Anstee J. W., The Bath-house at Low Borrow Bridge Fort, Tebay, *Contrebis* III, 76–85

Anstee, 1975b: An Aqueduct in the Tebay Gorge, *Contrebis* III, 74–75

Bird, 1977: Bird J., African Red Slip ware in Roman Britain, pp. 269–77, in Dore J. and Greene K. (eds), *Roman Pottery Studies in Britain and Beyond*, Oxford (BAR Suppl. No. 30)

Birley, 1936: Birley E. B., A Roman Altar from Bankshead; *CIL* VII, 802; *CW2* XXXVI, 1–7

Birley, 1946: Birley E. B., The Roman Site at Burrow-in-Lonsdale, *CW2* XLVI, 126–156

Birley, 1947: Birley E. B., The Roman Fort at Low Borrow Bridge, *CW2* XLVII, 1–19

Birley, 1953: Birley E. B., The Roman Milestone at Middleton in Lonsdale, *CW2* LIII, 52–63

Birley, 1958: Birley E. B., Two Lost Roman Inscriptions, *CW2* LVIII, 69–87

Birley, A, 1979: Birley A. R., *The People of Roman Britain*, London

Birley, R, 1977: Birley R. N., *Vindolanda: A Roman Frontier Post on Hadrians Wall*, London

Birley, R, 1989: Birley R. N, Vindolanda, *Current Archaeology*, 116

Bowen, 1972: Bowen E. G., *Britain and the Western Seaways*, London

Breeze, 1975: Breeze D. J., The Abandonment of the Antonine Wall: its date and implications, *Scot. Arch. Forum*, VII, 67–78

Breeze and Dobson, 1978: Breeze D. J. and Dobson B., *Hadrian's Wall*, Harmondsworth

Camden, 1610: Camden W., *Britannia*, (Philemon Holland's English translation)

Charlesworth, 1965: Charlesworth D., A Roman Milestone near Overtown, Lancs, *CW2* LXV, 427
Chippendall, 1933: Chippendall W. H., The Tatham Families of Burrow, Tunstall and Cantsfield, *CW2* XXXIII, 98–9
Collingwood, 1930: Collingwood R. G., Proceedings: Notes on the Roman fort at Overborough, *CW2* XXX, 216–17
Edwards, 1971: Edwards B. J. N., Roman Finds from 'Contrebis', *CW2* LXXI, 17–33
Edwards, 1977: Edwards B. J. N., in *LAB*, 3, 3
Ekwall, 1947: Ekwall E., *The Concise Oxford Dictionary of English Place-Names*, Oxford
Evans and Scull, 1990: Evans J. and Scull C., Field work on the Roman fort site at Blennerhasset, Cumbria, *CW2* XC, 127–137
Ewbank, 1960: Ewbank J. M., Cross-Section of the Roman Road in Casterton, Westmorland, *CW2* LX, 28–31
Ewbank, 1963: Ewbank J. M. (ed.), *Antiquary on Horseback*, Kendal
Ferguson, 1885: Ferguson R. S., The Roman Camp at Low Borrow Bridge, *CW1* VIII, 1–6
Fulford, 1989: Fulford M., Byzantium and Britain: a Mediterranean perspective on post-Roman Mediterranean Imports in Western Britain and Ireland, *Med. Arch.*, XXXIII, 1–6
Gemsege, 1759: Gemsege P., in *The Gentleman's Magazine*, XXIX, 407–8
Graystone, 1992: Graystone P., *Walking Roman Roads in Bowland*, Lancaster
Grimes, 1930: Grimes W. F., Holt, Denbighshire: The Works-Depot of the Twentieth Legion at Castle Lyons, *Y Cymmrodor* XLI
Higham, 1979: Higham N. J., An Aerial Survey of the Upper Lune Valley, pp. 31–8 in Higham N. J. (ed.), *The Changing Past*, Manchester
Higham, 1980: Higham N. J., Native Settlements West of the Pennines, pp. 41–7 in Branigan K. (ed.), *Rome and the Brigantes*, Sheffield
Higham, 1986: Higham N. J., *The Northern Counties to* A.D. *1000*, London
Higham and Jones, 1975: Higham N. J. and Jones G. D. B., Frontier, Forts and Farmers, *Arch. J.* CXXXII, 16–53
Higham and Jones, 1985: Higham N. J. and Jones G. D. B., *The Carvetii*, Gloucester
Hildyard and Gillam, 1951: Hildyard E. J. W. and Gillam J. P., Renewed Excavation at Low Borrow Bridge, *CW2* LI, 40–66
Hildyard, 1954: Hildyard E. J. W., Excavations at Burrow-in-Lonsdale, 1952–1953, *CW2* LIV, 66–101
Hind, 1977: Hind J. G. F., The 'Genounian' Part of Britain, *Britannia* VIII, 229–34
Howard-Davis, 1983–4: Howard-Davis C, Lancashire Sites and Monuments Record and its Computerisation, *Contrebis* XI, 3–25
Huckerby, Wells and Middleton, 1992: Huckerby E., Wells C. and Middleton R., Recent Palaeoecological and Archaeological Work in Over Wyre, Lancashire, pp. 9–18 in Middleton R. (ed.), *North-West Wetlands Survey: Annual Report, 1992*, Lancaster
Johnson, 1976: Johnson A. S., *The Roman Forts of the Saxon Shore*, London
Johnson, 1980: Johnson A. S., *Later Roman Britain*, London
Jones, 1974: Jones G. D. B., *Roman Manchester*, Altrincham
Jones, 1975: Jones G. D. B., The North-Western Interface, pp. 93–106 in Fowler P. J. (ed.), *Recent Work on Rural Archaeology*, Bradford-upon-Avon

Jones, 1982: Jones G. D. B., The Solway Frontier: Interim Report, 1976–81, *Britannia* XIII, 284–97

Jones and Shotter, 1988: Jones G. D. B. and Shotter D. C. A., *Roman Lancaster*, Manchester

Jones M. J., 1975: Jones M. J., *Roman Fort Defences to* A.D. *117*, Oxford, (BAR no. 21)

Lambert *et al.*, 1995: Lambert J., Hair N. J., Howard-Davis C. L. E., Newman R. H., and Oliver T. M., *Transect through Time*, Oxford

Leach, 1993: Leach R. H., The Roman Fort and *vicus* at Ambleside: Archaeological Research in 1982, *CW2* XCIII, 51–74

Leather, 1978: Leather G. M., *Lancaster Roman Bath-House*, Lancaster

Lewis, 1966: Lewis M. J. T., *Temples in Roman Britain*, Cambridge

Lowndes, 1963: Lowndes R. A. C., 'Celtic' Fields, farms and burial mounds in the Lune Valley, *CW2* LXIII, 77–95

Lowndes, 1964: Lowndes R. A. C., Excavation of a Romano-British Farmstead at Eller Beck, *CW2* LXIV, 1–13

Lukis, 1883: Lukis W. C. (ed.), *Stukeley's Diaries and Letters*, volume 2, Surtees Society, LXXVI

Macadam, 1964: Macadam E. M. L., A Section of the Roman Road south of Low Borrow Bridge, Westmorland, *CW2* LXIV, 76–80

MacGregor, 1976: MacGregor M., *Early Celtic Art in North Britain*, Leicester

Manning, 1975: Manning W. H., Economic Influences on land-use in the military areas of the Highland zone during the Roman period, pp. 112–16 in Evans J. G., Limbrey S., and Cleere H. (eds.), *The Effect of Man on the Landscape: the Highland Zone*, CBA Research Report, No. 11

Margary, 1973: Margary I. D., *Roman Roads in Britain*, London

Middleton, 1992: Middleton R., Field survey work in Lancashire, 1991–92, pp. 1–8 in Middleton R., (ed.), *North-West Wetlands Survey: Annual Report*, Lancaster

Moorhouse, 1912: Moorhouse A., Roman Altar at Tunstall, *CW2* XII, 431–2

North, 1951: North O. H., Roman Pottery from Burrow-in-Lonsdale, *CW2* LI, 178

North, 1953: North O. H., Excavations at Burrow-in-Lonsdale, 1952 and 1953, *CW2* LIII, 211–12

North, Hildyard and Gillam, 1948: North O. H., Hildyard E. J. W. and Gillam J. P., Trial Trenching at Burrow-in-Lonsdale, 1947, *CW2* XLVIII, 23–41

Nutton, 1968: Nutton V., A Greek Doctor at Chester, *Journal of the Chester Arch. Soc.*, LV, 7–13

Oldfield and Statham, 1964–5: Oldfield F. and Statham J. C., Stratigraphy and Pollen-analysis on Cockerham and Pilling Mosses, North Lancashire, *Manchester Memoirs* CVII, no. 6, 1–16

Park, 1990: Park C., (ed.), *Field Excursions in North-West England*, Milnthorpe

Penney, 1981: Penney S. H., *Lancaster: the Evolution of its Townscape to 1800*, Lancaster

Penney, 1983: Penney S. H., Romano-British Iron Extraction in North Lancashire, *CW2* LXXXIII, 59–61

von Petrikovits, 1971: von Petrikovits H., Fortifications in the North-Western Roman Empire from the third to the fifth centuries A.D., *JRS* LXI, 178–218

Potter, 1975: Potter T. W., Excavations at Burrow-in-Lonsdale, *CW2* LXXV, 376
Potter, 1979: Potter T. W., *The Romans in North-West England*, Kendal
Rauthmel, 1746, 1824: Rauthmel R., *The Roman Antiquities of Overborough*, Kirkby Lonsdale
Richmond, 1936: Richmond I. A., Roman Leaden Sealings from Brough-under-Stainmore, *CW2* XXXVI, 104–25
Rivet and Smith, 1979: Rivet A. L. F. and Smith C., *The Place-Names of Roman Britain*, London
Ross, 1916: Ross P., The Roman Road from Ribchester to Low Borrow Bridge (near Tebay), *Bradford Antiquary* VI, 243–66
Shotter, 1973: Shotter D. C. A., *Numeri Barcariorum*: a note on RIB 601, *Britannia* IV, 206–9
Shotter, 1978a: Shotter D. C. A., Three Early Imperial Hoards from Lancashire, *Coin Hoards* IV, 44–5
Shotter, 1978b: Shotter D. C. A., A Hoard of Antoniniani from Hackensall Hall Farm, *LAJ* I, 47–52
Shotter, 1980: Shotter D. C. A., The Roman Occupation of North-West England; the Coin-evidence, *CW2* LXXX, 1–15
Shotter, 1990: Shotter D. C. A., *Roman Coins from North-West England*, Lancaster
Shotter, 1993: Shotter D. C. A., *Romans and Britons in North-West England*, Lancaster
Shotter, 1994: Shotter D. C. A., Rome and the Brigantes: Early Hostilities, *CW2* XCIV, 21–34
Shotter, 1995: Shotter D. C. A., Romans in South Cumbria: a note, *CW2* XCV, (forthcoming)
Shotter and White, 1990: Shotter D. C. A. and White A. J., *The Roman Fort and Town of Lancaster*, Lancaster
Swain, 1992: Swain R., *Walking Down the Lune*, Milnthorpe
Terry, 1802: Terry M., in *The Gentleman's Magazine*, LXXII, 993 and Pl. I. 7
Thomas, 1959: Thomas C., Imported Pottery in Dark-Age Western Britain, *Med. Arch.*, III, 89–111
Thomas, 1971: Thomas C., *The Early Christian Archaeology of North Britain*, Glasgow
Toulmin-Smith, 1910: Toulmin-Smith L., *The Itinerary of John Leland . . .*, (5 vols), London
Villy, 1937: Villy F., The Roman Road north-west from Overborough, *CW2* XXXVII, 49
Watkin, 1883: Watkin W. T., *Roman Lancashire*, Liverpool
Webster, 1971: Webster R. A., A morphological study of Romano-British settlements in Westmorland, *CW2* LXXI, 64–74
White, 1974: White A. J., Excavations in the vicus, Lancaster, 1973–4, *Contrebis* II, 2, 16–20
White, 1975: White A. J., Excavations at No. 1 Penny Street, Lancaster, *Contrebis* III. 1, 30–33
White, 1976: White A. J., The Wery Wall – some comments, *Contrebis* IV, 24
White, 1993: White A. J., (ed.), *A History of Lancaster 1193–1993*, Keele
Wright, 1954: Wright R. P., The Inscriptions, p. 97 in Hildyard, 1954
Yates, 1851: Yates J., Additional Observations on the Bulla worn by Roman boys, *Arch. J.* VIII, 166–71